Andrzej Heyduk

Postcards from "Paradise"

ISBN: 978-1-0881-5419-9

Hire-a-Geek LLC

Front cover design: Jacek Szatkowski

This book is not my autobiography, although at times it may seem to be, as it is a first person narrative. First of all, it mostly covers only the period from 1963 to 1983. More importantly, it would be presumptuous and just silly for me to attempt something like that, because in the public sphere I am practically a nobody. However, I lived through some turbulent times during which I progressed from being a totally subjugated citizen of an oppressive country to a largely free spirit.

This was not an easy transition, but it was also fascinating because of all kinds of twists and turns. My story is not unique, although it is a bit unusual. I decided to share it, because sooner all later all of this will succumb to oblivion. History will continue telling the tale of the rise and fall of communism, but it will do it on a grand scale. My account is totally different - it is a series of images, or flashbacks, or "postcards", illustrating life under totalitarianism on a personal, local level. It obviously relies on my own circumstances and my own life, because I have no other points of reference.

But this is not my story. It is the story of millions of people who lived in the communist bloc - not by choice, but by happenstance - and who not only survived, but successfully resisted years of mind-numbing, omnipresent indoctrination and repression. There are countless versions of this story, and this one is mine.

Andrzej, Fort Wayne, 9th of September 2023

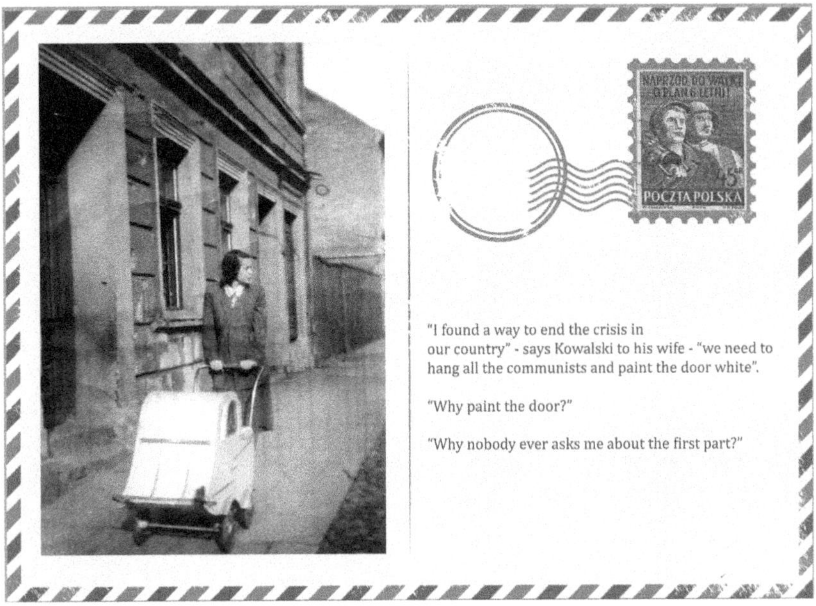
NAPRZÓD DO WALKI
O PLAN 6 LETNI
POCZTA POLSKA
"I found a way to end the crisis in our country" - says Kowalski to his wife - "we need to hang all the communists and paint the door white".
"Why paint the door?"
"Why nobody ever asks me about the first part?"

Postcard no. 1 - Ingress

I was born in 1953, emerging upon this world not in a hospital, but at the home of my parents, in a small town situated in the southwestern corner of Poland. Except it wasn't just Poland. It was People's Republic of Poland, usually referred to as PRL. It was supposed to be a proletarian paradise, created by a bunch of ill-educated, boorish communist thugs, who after World War II were „imported" from Moscow and established a puppet government that was to last for over 4 decades.

Needless to say, on that December day of 1953 I couldn't care less about the uncertain realities of my very early life. Nor was I particularly interested in the fact that just a few months earlier Joseph Stalin had thankfully kicked the bucket. Unbeknownst to me, my parents were already plotting a move to a big city just 50 miles to the south where my father got a managerial job. Before the war this city was called Breslau and was home to over 700 thousand Germans. But now it was Wrocław, a newly acquired Polish city, a part of the so-called Regained Territories. „Uncle Joe", before he departed for hell, had convinced his Western allies at the conference in Potsdam that Poland should be rewarded with a large sliver of western Germany in exchange of an equally large sliver of eastern Poland taken over by the Russians.

While Poland moved west, in 1955 my family moved south. At that time Wrocław was a weird place. All the Germans were gone, first forced by the Nazis to march out of the city in the bitter cold of 1945 winter, and then a few years later the stragglers were forcibly shipped westward by Stalin's henchmen. Ruins were still everywhere, but my family moved into a brand new, neo-Stalinist apartment block in the city center. Life was relatively good. As a young child I never suffered any material hardships and had a happy, well-protected childhood, together with my two siblings, Jola and Tomek.

What I could not have known was the fact that I was born into a totalitarian society in which every aspect of everyone's life was tightly controlled by the communist government. People were supposed to live in the permanent state of subsistence - the misery of everyday life was not painful enough to cause social unrest, but was too strong to offer any excessive comfort or happiness to anyone but governmental dignitaries.

I started my life in a country fast converting from Nazi fascism to Soviet communism. In a number of ways this transition was easy. For example, the new state security and police forces in Wrocław moved into an imposing, gloomy red brick building which just a few years earlier was used by the Gestapo. The respective ideologies were different, if only marginally, but the shrieks and cries of the interrogated people remained the same.

In my preschool years I traveled frequently with my parents back to my home town of Zduny to visit my grandfather Sylwester and grandmother Maria. These trips were fraught with unintended symbolism. Before the war this small town lied just a mile and a half away from the Polish-German border on the other side of which was the equally small German town of Freyhan. My father Wacław often told me prewar stories about the intimate connections between these two communities - there were family ties, social ties, drinking ties, and even joint mushroom picking ties. All of that suddenly disappeared in the late thirties as the Hitler mania overran sanity. Families which lived side by side for generations in peace and relative prosperity became enemies, very much like Serbs and Croats, Catholics and Protestants, or Beatles and Rolling Stones fans. Humans will never learn.

Whenever I and my family were traveling to Zduny, my father would always point out that right outside of Cieszków (formerly Freyhan) there was a row of flat houses which used to house customs and border control personnel. Now it was all one country - no passports, no controls, and no Germans.

Grandfather Sylwester was a towering presence - tall, serious, sometimes almost menacing. He looked somewhat like general Charles de Gaulle in retirement. Before the war he was briefly deputy mayor of Zduny. When in 1948 the Polish communists, organizing and rigging first post-war parliamentary elections, asked him to participate, he reportedly told them to go and fuck themselves. Sadly, they didn't. He spent the next two decades of his life listening to Radio Free Europe in his darkened study. Back then I had no idea what Radio Free Europe was and why anybody would listen to it. As far as I was concerned, my grandfather was just a bit strange and remote. I didn't have any meaningful relationship with him. We met, but rarely talked. Sylwester was a distant, reclusive figure who was extremely ill-suited to People's Republic of Poland. It would take the next decade for me to understand that it wasn't my grandfather who was weird. It was the reality in which he had to live.

On one occasion, some time in early sixties, Sylwester suddenly walked into the sitting room of his house with a small briefcase in his hand.

„I have a surprise for you" - he said to me and my two siblings.

„What is it?" - I asked excitedly.

He opened the briefcase. Inside there were rows of banknotes, neatly wrapped in currency straps. It was money issued in prewar Poland. His stash, apparently put away years earlier for a rainy day, was completely worthless, and therefore very good as play money. It seemed he offered his grandchildren a toy in the form of the last remaining, material link to the „good old days". He was done. His Poland was done. A couple of years later his life was done.

Unfortunately for millions of Poles, the new reality was very far away from being done. As I approached school years, I sometimes saw things which caused fleeting puzzlement, even at a very young age. From my parents' apartment on the 4th floor I had a good view of the bombed out building, reduced to rubble at the end of the war. I often played in these ruins with my neighborhood buddies and occasionally found broken kitchen tiles with German inscriptions, bent spoons, book fragments, pieces of furniture, utensils, half-destroyed photographs, and maps. These were all mementos of someone's shattered existence, of someone's life in the city of Breslau. Eventually two big excavators showed up and removed all the debris. A bit later an ugly, gray, boxy apartment block was built in the same spot.

In those days there was a lot of propaganda concerning "Regained Territories". Ignoring the fact that the Germans lived in Breslau for over 7 hundred years, the communists eagerly spread the false narrative according to which Wrocław was an ancient Polish city which finally returned to its proper place within the borders of Poland. The town called Vratislavia was Polish for a couple of centuries in medieval times. After the war, as soon as the first Polish administration was in place, the campaign to remove all traces of the Germans started. All the street names were changed, monuments destroyed, and some buildings, viewed as too "Teutonic", were razed to the ground. The very name Breslau became taboo, and was not supposed to be used.

"Correcting" history was one of the favorite activities of the new rulers. They did it often and with insolent gusto. Whatever was not within the parameters of the new communist reality had to be changed or simply eradicated. As a young kid I was totally unaware of any of this. As far as I was concerned, I simply lived in a town called Wrocław. It didn't matter whether it was regained, stolen or just taken over.

I was also oblivious to the fact that in the years 1945-55 the city witnessed one of the largest human migrations of that time. Seven hundred thousand Germans died, were killed or got shipped west by Stalin, and a few hundred thousand Poles from Lwów and its vicinity (today Lviv in Ukraine) were kicked out of their homes and told to go to "new" Poland. Most of them ended up in Lower Silesia where Wrocław was trying to re-imagine itself as a Polish city. There were no real winners in all of that. The lives of thousands of people had been uprooted on the whim of allied powers, carving up new Europe at the Potsdam Conference.

When I first got to Wrocław in 1955, the city was so full of refugees from Lwów, called Lwowiacy, that their peculiar, charming accent was heard everywhere. A lot of them were professors, teachers, writers, journalists, actors, and artists. Some brought with them their customs and cuisine. The villages in Lower Silesia were almost all settled by an influx of peasants from eastern Poland - the part of the country that unexpectedly became Soviet Union. But of course I didn't know about any of this back then.

From the diary of a communist:

First day: I switch the radio on - Lenin

Second day: I read a newspaper - Lenin

Third day: I look at posters - Lenin

Fourth day: I'm afraid to open a can of peas

Postcard no. 2 - Inklings of autocracy

POZDRAWIAMY KOBIETY
PRACUJĄCE DLA POKOJU
I ROZKWITU OJCZYZNY!

L iving in a totalitarian state usually doesn't matter a lot to young kids. They go to kindergarten and then enter their primary schools, blissfully oblivious of the bullshit world of their elders. It didn't matter to me that my country was on the eastern side of the post-war European divide, and therefore alienated, anachronistic and not very prosperous. It didn't matter that there was only one „correct" view of the world, according to which the good guys were Kremlin stooges and the rest of the world was full of blood-thirsty imperialists.

And yet it was impossible to be completely isolated from the surrounding totalitarian nonsense. Whether one wanted or not, it was necessary to participate one way or the other in this lame society. People had to go to schools run by the government, use the public health system, listen to daily propaganda in the media, and go to work. You could not trudge through knee-deep shit without getting dirty and smelly.

I didn't understand why my school curriculum included mandatory Russian language courses. Nor did I understand the need for having „civic classes" during which various despondent teachers were extolling the virtues of socialism and praising the enormous successes of Poland's „big brother" to the east. I knew, and was frequently told, that somewhere out there, in the west, there were enemies of my country and my way of life, such as it was. There were American imperialists. There were Germans dreaming of retaking their lost land. And there were Zionists, although I had trouble figuring out who exactly they were and why they were a threat.

During family dinners my mother Zofia sometimes

mentioned the subject of „Germans returning".

„What if they show up and throw us out?" - she would say.

„Nobody is returning" - my father would respond - „It's over. The Germans are out of here forever".

„But what if they do?" - persisted Zofia.

She wasn't alone in her doubts. Many new inhabitants of Wrocław treated their city as a temporary transit point, as something that will not last for long. Such feelings were reinforced by the fact the in the first few years after the war a lot of half-destroyed buildings were demolished, so that the bricks recovered from them could be shipped to Warsaw. The Polish capital was also in ruins, and its rebuilding was given top priority. Wrocław was a part of "Regained Territories", but initially served as a source of building materials.

However, those who thought that the Polish presence in the city would only be temporary were mistaken. Wrocław remains in Poland and today is much more Polish than ever before. But for more or less two decades after the war it was almost like a Polish version of the Wild West. Once the ruins were cleared, there were vast barren spaces in the middle of the city. Before the war they were densely populated areas which got totally obliterated in the spring of 1945. There were also areas where the ruins persisted and became very shady places, like the so-called „Małpi Gaj" (Monkey Grove), full of drunks, teenage troublemakers and whores.

In 1962 there was suddenly a new subject at the dinner table. My parents discussed, usually in subdued, quiet voices, the possibility of a new war breaking out. A nuclear one. Something ominous was in the air, but official media said nothing, and only people like grandfather Sylwester, listening to the radio in his darkened study, heard of the so-called Cuban missile crisis. Various rumors spread like wildfire and people started buying vast quantities of salt. I was scared, although I didn't know of what, and I thought that the salt buying spree was plain silly unless everybody wanted to eat pretty salty food just before dying. For the first time in my short life I started wondering about the fact that there was a widening gap between official news, stark everyday realities, and unofficial gossip.

Various doubts in my mind slowly grew and became stronger. In early 1968 there were widespread student strikes and riots all over Poland. The response of the government was heavy-handed and for some inexplicable reason depended on blaming everything on Zionists, i.e. Jews, who were being coerced into leaving Poland. It was quite possible that I had some Jewish friends, but I was not aware of that and never thought there was any „Jewish problem" in my country. My Polish teacher and Auschwitz survivor was a Jew, but she was a problem only unto herself - in sporadic fits of rage she would beat her daughter in front of the whole class. Somehow nobody questioned this behavior and pretended that everything was just fine.

The events of 1968 puzzled me. Suddenly Polish television was full of reports from „spontaneous rallies" of workers who carried big signs saying things like „Zionists go to Israel" or „Cleanse the party from Zionist elements". But who or what the fuck were Zionist elements? And why should they go to Israel? I didn't know, but I did know that prior to 1968 nobody mentioned any of this in public.

There was another major event in the same year. Soviet tanks (and some Polish ones too) rolled into Czechoslovakia to squash something called the Prague Spring, a pro-democracy movement. This was a shameful intervention which even to a 15-year old kid seemed totally senseless and unjustified. Something was decidedly wrong with the proletarian paradise. My parents and various members of my family were openly critical of the brutal Soviet move, even though normally they avoided talking about politics, mainly because it was totally pointless. In communist Poland being critical of the government was only possible within the confines of one's home. It was not uncommon for the entire family to gather around a black-and-white TV set to watch the nightly news and openly laugh at all the lies, stupid propaganda, and promises of future wealth and happiness once "true socialism" was attained. However, no one – with the exception of a small number of brave dissidents – would dare laugh at such things in public.

My early school years were largely uneventful. I was a puny kid with flaming red hair and a myriad of freckles. In fact, I always looked about two years younger than my peers. This meant that I was an easy target of school bullies and frequent subject of jokes and derisive comments. All of this could have resulted in my becoming a serial killer or a sex pervert or both. However, I wisely chose a different career path, becoming a good student and voracious reader. Half way through my elementary school my parents signed me up for voluntary English classes, in addition to the mandatory Russian ones. I didn't know that at the time, but it was a development which would turn out to be of monumental importance.

Why don't communists ever go to hell?

Because they would build such a paradise there that all the devils would immediately flee.

Postcard no. 3 - The absence of God

Although the reds were in full control in Poland, there was one institution which they never dared to touch - the Catholic church. With a population which had been historically deeply religious it was too risky for the authorities to challenge the church hierarchy or resort to any open form of persecution. The priests operated under difficult circumstances, but retained a lot of independence.

As a result, the country existed in a schizophrenic state. There was a vast, state bureaucracy with all its rules and ideological prescriptions. The ruling communist party (called PZPR) was in control, but only a relatively small percentage of the population were formally members. My father was a member, because - like a lot of other Poles - he had to sign up in order to be employed in his position. He couldn't care less about Marx and Engels. He didn't want his children to be communists. And he followed deeply-rooted religious traditions which had absolutely nothing to do with the people in power, although faith was probably not a big factor in his life. Almost everybody in the distorted reality of PRL still attended church every Sunday, participated in religious activities, baptized their children, and sent them to First Communion.

The duality of ideology in Poland was most obvious in the case of marriages. The only legal way of getting married was to go through a totally secular procedure in front of a government bureaucrat, but almost all newlyweds also had a church ceremony which by itself was not legally binding. This was particularly awkward in the case of party officials who in their daily life professed Marxist inspired atheism, but then attended their sons' or daughters' church weddings, usually trying desperately to keep it a secret.

The Catholic church offered a tenuous refuge from a philosophy which was totally alien to most of Poles. It was the only alternative for decades. Some relatively independent public opinion polls in 1948, just before the rigged parliamentary elections, indicated that in a free and open vote the communists could have counted on less than 5% of the vote. It wasn't a surprise in a country which was over 90% Catholic. Religion was always a very important part of postwar Polish society, despite decades of secular propaganda.

For me there was one major problem with all of that - I didn't believe in God. In fact much later, when reflecting on my past, I couldn't remember ever being religious in any sense, even for a moment. I thought all the biblical stories were just plain silly, and the story of creation seemed to be ludicrous. In particular, even at a pretty young age I wondered, as countless others have throughout ages, why God had to take six days to create the universe if he was omnipotent and could have done it all in a minute. And why did he have to rest on the seventh day? Today I know that numerous biblical scholars have all kinds of explanations for that, none of which make any sense to me, not to mention the fact that any such discussions actually presuppose God's existence. But back then I was just looking at this stuff from the point of view of a dubious adolescent.

My mother sent me and my younger brother Tomek to church every Sunday, but very quickly I started detesting this experience and came to the conclusion that all of that was a big hoax, designed to control people and scare them into obedience. This was unsettling, because in large measure the communists were trying to do exactly the same thing, although using a dramatically different ideology.

After a while I stopped going to church altogether - instead I went with my brother to a cafe to have tea. Our mother for years had no idea this was happening. Unfortunately it was much more tricky to extricate myself from religious education. Teaching religion in public schools was forbidden, but churches were allowed to offer religious classes at their parish facilities. So I was signed up for such classes by my parents, and because attendance was being checked, it was impossible to cheat your way out of it.

For about 3 years I attended my alternative, religious school where sister Maria, in the typical penguin regalia of a Catholic nun, instilled fear in young kids by warning them about hell and damnation, which apparently awaited all the sinners. And although corporal punishment was technically not allowed, sister Maria often had a wooden ruler in her hand which she used to smack the hands of misbehaving students.

I was not scared of sister Maria. This was primarily due to the fact that she was an attractive, shapely woman in her late twenties, and in my nascent sexuality I spent quite a lot of time imagining how she would look without the penguin garb, preferably without clothing of any kind. I also knew that she couldn't smack my dirty thoughts with her ruler. As long as I went to church, I also had to go to confession every now and then, which to me was one of the stupidest aspects of Catholicism. Since I never wanted to share my sins with a fat priest who for some reason was supposed to be a direct link to non-existent God, I typically invented a short list of relatively benign sins to just get off the hook. Obviously, it never occurred to me to confess that what I really wanted to do was to disrobe sister Maria. Basically, I wanted her to kick the habit.

Postcard no. 4 - Spittle-covered dwarves

Indoctrination of any kind, however stupid, can be insidious and treacherous. In communist Poland it was essentially the art of repeating the same lies over and over again so that sooner or later people started believing that at least part of this bullshit was true. It was impossible for me, or anybody else for that matter, to avoid the steady stream of disinformation and falsehoods. This stuff was everywhere - media, schools, public discussions, and even family gatherings. As an elementary school student I never seriously questioned any of this. I was a part of a totally fucked-up society, and I didn't really know about it. I had no other points of reference and no independent sources of information. Like all my compatriots, I could have spent the rest of my life in this state of idiotic ignorance.

Poland was not North Korea. Its isolation from the western world was obvious, but not total. It was possible to learn about things that the government didn't want people to be aware of, and two Polish language radio stations - Free Europe and Voice of America - could be listened to, even though from to time their transmissions were being jammed. There was also access to Western music, movies, and art as long as none of this breached the prescribed norms. However, most people didn't bother to seek independent news and lived in the cocoon created for them by the authorities.

All of this was happening in the "dark ages", i.e. in the year 20 BI (before Internet). While today email, social media, and instant messages make the task of isolating any nation from the world a difficult proposition, in the 60s and 70s tin pot dictators were usually pretty effective in controlling their hapless victims. By the same token, peering through the isolation was hard and often required a lot of ingenuity and perseverance.

One of the more stealthy ways in which the communists were molding society to their liking was through teaching total falsehoods in schools. It was especially prevalent in the case of history which in the books given to students was distorted beyond recognition. One of the most glaring examples of that was the treatment of underground movements in Poland under Nazi occupation. Home Army (Armia Krajowa or AK)), supported by the Polish government in exile residing in London, was one of the largest organizations of that kind in Europe, and by the end of 1944 had roughly 400 thousand active fighters. AK organized countless attacks on German personnel, train transports, supply lines, etc. It also tried to shield Poles from German persecution, although very often that was simply impossible. AK operated with incredible ingenuity and resourcefulness, creating what in effect amounted to the conspiratorial Polish state with its own army, schools, institutions, administration, etc.

However, this was not what kids were being taught in schools. AK was barely mentioned and characterized as small, ineffective, passive, and „reactionary", whatever the hell that meant. Students learned that the biggest and most important underground organization during WWII was Armia Ludowa (People's Army or AL), and the books were full of supposedly incredible success stories of this formation. In reality, AL was more than 10 times smaller than AK, and was only created in 1944 on the initiative of the Kremlin. It cannot be denied that the fighters of AL did engage the Nazis, but their influence was pretty small. In fact, AL was created only because Stalin needed some force friendly to the Soviets once they found themselves in Poland. It was one of the first steps towards future subjugation of the country.

As soon as the war was over, AL morphed into first communist administration cells, while members of AK, especially high ranking commanders, were persecuted, imprisoned, shipped off to Siberia or simply executed. The official story in PRL was that heroic soldiers of AL played a huge part in the liberation of Poland, aiding the Red Army in their march towards Berlin.

In 1945 the communists distributed a shameful poster showing a soldier of AL towering over a little, furious guy with an AK placard on his neck. The image bore a slogan: "Olbrzym i zapluty karzeł reakcji". It is difficult to translate this, but more or less it says "A giant and a spittle-covered dwarf of reactionary forces". It is even more difficult to decipher what the slogan actually meant. It was obviously an attempt to belittle the fighters of AK and to portray them as pitiful gnomes, representing the backward forces of prewar Poland, i.e. capitalism and democracy.

The poster was such a disgustingly blatant and offensive lie that it was removed from circulation relatively quickly. But the phraseology stuck and was later used often against the enemies of the government, real or perceived. In fact, anybody who criticized the government in any way almost automatically qualified as being a spittle-covered dwarf. But it wasn't the only term to describe enemies of the new order. Sometimes a party official betrayed "rightist-nationalist deviations", which usually meant disciplinary action of some sort for unspecified transgressions. Some people were called "revisionists", and some others - "class enemies". And of course the nation was full of "imperialist lackeys" and "sworn enemies of the socialist motherland".

Another lie sold in Polish schools concerned the mass execution of nearly 22 thousand Polish POWs, mostly officers, on direct orders from Stalin, issued in 1940. Typically people were killed with a single shot to the back of their heads, and most of the killings occurred in the Katyń forest near the Russian city of Smolensk. The name of this forest became a taboo subject for Polish and Soviet communists. Initially Stalin and his gang tried to pin the murders on the Germans, but this was so ridiculously false that after a while it was decided that the massacre would never be mentioned in any public sphere, including schools. So technically it wasn't a lie, but suppression of the truth.

As a result, I never learned in school either about AK or

Katyń massacre. Sometimes subjects like this were mentioned in various conversations. Also, I had a friend in high school, Maciek, who came from an aristocratic family and whose parents knew much more about this than an average Polish student. It didn't change the fact that the young generation educated in PRL came out of schools with an often distorted view of their country's history.

Westerners often wonder why people living in totalitarian states don't revolt and overthrow their rulers. The answer is fairly simple. First, the numbing constant indoctrination renders a large part of society apathetic and susceptible to accepting even the most blatant falsehoods. People simply don't know that their lives are screwed up and that it is possible to have a completely different existence. Second, in order to revolt and protest, and especially fight in the streets, the populace has to be driven to utter desperation and must have absolutely nothing to lose. Eventually that did happen in Poland, but it took 27 years of my life for my country to reach that point. It would be fair to say that for the first 15 years of this time I was more or less a dutiful participant of the totalitarian mediocrity surrounding me.

Sometimes people in the West also have a mistaken view that living in an oppressive society means constant suffering, fear, deprivation, and hopelessness. Nothing can be further from the truth. People in communist Poland lived vibrant, joyous, private lives. They enjoyed family and friends, went to parties, cherished the arts, engaged in age-old activities such as excessive drinking, hunting or mushroom picking, and were more or less a pretty happy bunch. But this happiness stopped at the border line between what was private and what was official.

In the 60. the *de facto* ruler of Poland was Władysław Gomułka, the first secretary of PZPR, who would have been almost a comical figure, were it not for the fact that at any particular time he could have done anything that he wanted as long as it wasn't against the wishes of his masters in Moscow. He was a really dumb ideologue who had the habit of delivering excruciatingly long speeches in which he invariably boasted about the fictitious successes of the Polish economy, such as the ever increasing number of cattle being raised and the vast amounts of wheat being harvested. He was almost universally ignored and ridiculed.

The communists celebrated with particular zeal May Day, i.e. the 1st of May which was designated as the "Labor Holiday". There were street parades full of people carrying large placards with painfully stupid slogans. There were open air festivities of all sorts. And there were speeches by party leaders, usually assembled on large podiums, overlooking the marching masses. Some people, like my father, had to attend these farcical events, because attendance was required. A lot of other Poles showed up, because it was a free day in early spring, so if the weather was good, people actually had lots of fun, although they did not necessarily associate the merriment with Marx and Engels. In my childhood I also enjoyed this day and didn't bother too much to find out why marching workers carried signs saying things like "Long live the party" or "We greet the great Soviet nation". This was the language of totalitarianism, but I was being increasingly attracted to a totally different language.

After I entered high school, I continued my English education and by the age of 16 I became proficient enough to be able to read and understand almost any English text, although I couldn't speak the language fluently. The flood gates were about to be breached. One of the reasons for that was that the communist apparatus essentially assumed that they ruled mostly stupid people who could be easily and endlessly manipulated. They also assumed that nobody in Poland really knew any foreign languages beyond those taught in meaningless and useless German or Latin courses, not to mention the Russian ones. They were wrong.

While Polish media were tightly controlled and censored, it was possible to walk into a facility called International Book and Press Club and read freely relatively recent copies of „Newsweek" or „The Times". This was „English stuff", linguistically inaccessible to the general populace, and therefore nobody in the upper echelons of power gave a shit.

But I did. Suddenly I was awash with independent news from all over the world. I became aware of the Watergate scandal, even though it was never really reported on in Poland. I found out that the „imperialist" war in Vietnam was actually a proxy war between Russia and USA. I could read countless independent texts about AK, AL, and the events in Katyń forest. And I suddenly knew about the fact that I lived in an isolated, pitiful Warsaw Pact country from which there was virtually no escape. I was now able to join my grandfather's reality without listening to Radio Free Europe.

All of this was of enormous importance. I began to understand that knowing English gave me in essence the same power as mythical Prometheus had over Zeus. Prometheus stole fire from the Greek gods to give it to humanity in the form of technology, rationalism, and knowledge. He was cruelly punished, but eventually emerged as a symbol of victory of reason over autocracy, and one of his weapons against Zeus was the mastery of linguistic expression. I didn't know that yet, but this ancient Greek drama would play an important part in my life a bit later. I was not able to fight the autocracy of the rulers of my own country, at least not yet, but my linguistic assent was synonymous with obtaining powers that only few of my compatriots could then achieve. I was - in effect - a sprouting spittle-covered dwarf of reactionary forces.

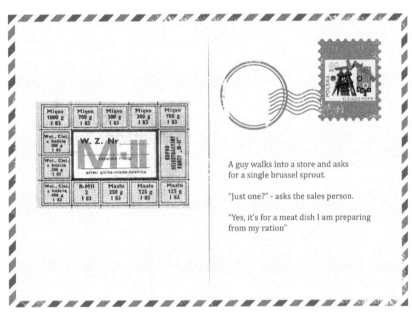

A guy walks into a store and asks for a single brussel sprout.

"Just one?" - asks the sales person.

"Yes, it's for a meat dish I am preparing from my ration"

Postcard no. 5 - Rationed life

After high school I decided to study English and linguistics at the University of Wrocław. It was an odd choice, because it didn't usually result in a meaningful professional career other than that of a provincial school teacher. But I was already somewhat intoxicated by the prospect of fully mastering English. And I did just that. Half way through my college years I acquired native-like fluency in the speech of Anglo-Saxons. I was also engrossed in English literature and culture. Additionally, I got to know, on a personal level, a few of my American and British teachers who worked on contracts at my university. In particular, I became close friends with Peter and his wife Jean, a married couple from Scotland who worked for an organization called The British Council. Thanks to them spoken English was suddenly transplanted from a classroom context to everyday life - idle chats at dinner tables, free-wheeling conversations about virtually anything, silly arguments, jokes, political discussions, etc.

The profound consequence of all of this was that my mind became a weirdly transitional entity. The baggage of two decades of communist indoctrination was still there and it was difficult to discard, but at the same time there was a steady and increasing flow of independent information which clashed dramatically with the reality of the PRL world. And that reality was becoming increasingly difficult to rationally explain.

Speaking of indoctrination, while college education in PRL was free and usually of high standard, all students had to take two mandatory courses - political economy (i.e. communist propaganda), and Marxist philosophy (i.e. more communist propaganda). This was regardless of what one's major area of studies was. I excelled at these two subjects, primarily because of my incredible ability to spontaneously spew bullshit which had no basis in any real knowledge, but sounded coherent. By the time I had to take these courses I knew very well they were total and unnecessary rubbish.

In December of 1970, after the authorities announced price increases for all major food types, shipyard workers in the city of Gdańsk went on strike and then marched through the streets. The rulers didn't take to this rebellion very kindly. The revolt was brutally suppressed, with many striking workers shot dead. The shock of these events, which were barely reported by the official media, forced PZPR to ditch Gomułka and install Edward Gierek, a younger and much more likable character. However, the change of leadership didn't matter. These people were all just lackeys of the Kremlin and in that sense were totally powerless. In early 70. things got a bit better in Poland, primarily because of borrowing vast amounts of money from the West. But then everything descended into the usual spiral of economic and political hopelessness.

The height of this decline was the rationing system. By mid-seventies stores were basically empty - they had nothing to sell and their personnel stood idly by the barren shelves, usually with bored or disgruntled looks on their faces. Initially the shortages applied to some basic foodstuffs, like sugar and butter, but then expanded to virtually anything one would need to lead a normal life - meat, coffee, tea, bread, flour, potatoes, vegetables, cooking oil, milk, salt, vinegar, matches, soap, baby diapers, toilet paper, and some clothing, such as underwear.

All of this rationing was invariably explained by the authorities as „temporary problems with supplying the market". But everybody knew that the Polish economy was basically in shambles and there was no clear prospect of improvement any time soon. All the Poles, except for the few privileged individuals, were being humiliated almost every day by not having regular access to basic commodities. Having the ration coupons the government issued didn't actually guarantee that the rationed item would be available. It was all a total crap shoot.

One day I was in the city of Jelenia Góra, south of Wrocław, where I worked with some friends on a theater festival bulletin called „Jeleń Teatralny". On request from a smoking member of the editorial crew I went to a nearby newsstand to buy some matches. When I got there, the following conversation took place:

„Hi, can I have a box of matches?"

„We don't have any matches."

„Really? When will you have matches?"

„We will never have any matches anymore."

The newsstand guy instantly became philosopher of the day, at least in my eyes.

The tragicomic surrealism of all this was not lost on the populace. There were countless jokes about the rationing system, the dumb government propaganda, the abject silliness of the communist system, etc. One of the jokes ran like this:

„Did you get your ration coupon for women's panties?"

„I tried, but they told me that only women working on high ladders in short skirts could get those."

Some Poles lived largely outside of this everyday struggle. The PZPR echelons had their own stores, inaccessible to the „proletariat", where things were usually abundant. And those lucky individuals who had access to western currencies could use special stores, called „Pewex", where for dollars, pounds and francs one could buy more or less the stuff available in an average shop in Germany, France or US. The very existence of „Pewex" was a tacit admission on the part of the communists that the Polish currency was totally worthless and that the country sanctioned a weird dual reality in which the vast majority of the population lived in the constant state of economic impoverishment while a tiny minority enjoyed a mock-up of western standards.

All kinds of goods were available on the black market, which in the late 70. had become vast, but prices were usually exorbitant. People in Poland were doomed to stand in long lines for virtually anything - from coffee and toilet paper to furniture and shoes. Speaking of toilet paper, in PRL it became a priceless item for which people hunted for hours or even days. The lucky individuals who managed to buy it paraded triumphantly with their rings of *Scheisspapier* strung around their necks. The unlucky individuals could always use sheets cut out of „Pravda" newspapers, but that was both good and bad. The good thing was that you could wipe your ass with a picture of Leonid Brezhnev. The bad thing was that the print ink was of poor quality and easily smeared.

Poles wasted countless hours trying to buy stuff which was available only from time to time or not at all. Citrus fruit, like oranges and lemons, were in stores only once a year - before Christmas. Usually they graced the shelves for just a few hours and were immediately sold out. The oranges, by the way, were usually imported from Cuba - they were greenish and bitter, but that was better than nothing. The grateful nation sometimes referred to them as "Fidel's balls". Gin was sometimes available, but usually not tonic, or the other way round, so making a classic drink was typically a waiting game. However vodka was available almost all the time - the nation needed to be properly "lubricated" and kept in a docile frame of mind.

In fact any shopping in PRL was a matter of luck. Usually there was nothing in the stores, but every now and then one would chance upon a shop which just got a „dostawa" (delivery) of something. It didn't matter what it was - people would immediately form a line, sometimes not knowing what was being sold. Since everything was in short supply, whatever was delivered was automatically desired. There was an expression in Polish which neatly summed it all up. Goods were not really delivered to the stores. They were dropped. Typically one would say something like „dziś rzucili pomarańcze" which literally meant „today they dropped oranges". They, the people in power, were dropping scraps onto the market, and the nation was supposed to be grateful and happy.

Poles had to bear constant material misery and -

unfortunately - to some extent they got used to it. Hunger was never a real threat, but only few people seriously questioned the fact that life in the country was difficult, and no one openly asked why in other parts of the world, supposedly full of oppressive capitalists and suffering proletariat, people didn't have to stand in line for two hours to get some scraps of meat. The food ration coupons became a part of the fabric of everyday life, and with time people stopped seeing them as anything unusual.

The vast majority of the Polish population back then never traveled to the West. A few American TV series were being shown, for example „Kojak", so obviously it was possible to see that the New York City police lieutenant sometimes walked into stores which were bursting with all kinds of goods. Polish TV viewers could also see that New Yorkers didn't wait in lines for anything. But it was all a different world, an alternate and unreachable reality where Telly Savalas as a policeman would routinely ask "Who loves ya, baby?" while sucking on his lollipop. And for most Poles it was just a show, not a real world.

A passenger ship was overloaded and sinking. The captain asked his first officer to convince people to jump off into the ocean. After a while he asked him how it went.

"It went well. I told the Englishmen that real gentlemen would jump. I appealed to the patriotism of the Frenchmen, and they jumped. I told the Russians that there was no more vodka on board, and they jumped. It was a bit difficult with the Poles, but they jumped once I told them that jumping off the ship was strictly forbidden".

Postcard no. 6 - The miracle of Sue

In 1973 I went to the city of Poznań to participate in the Summer English Camp, an event organized by my university. The idea was to get the students to mix in an informal context with a bunch of English teachers, mostly Britons invited to Poland just for this occasion. It was a very interesting idea since direct contacts between students of English and native speakers of the language were a rarity. Apart from classes there were various other events such as theater performances, dances, linguistic workshops, etc.

It was in Poznań that I first met a young Welsh teacher, Sue, who back home in London taught English to foreigners from all over the world. Our meeting was a fleeting moment of no immediate consequence. However, when I went back to Wrocław, I got a call from Sue's accidental friend, a somewhat wild American teacher, who explained that the two of them had decided to travel a bit around Poland and were going to come to my city and stay for a couple of days.

At that time I already suspected that all contacts with western foreigners were somehow being monitored by Służba Bezpieczeństwa (SB), the Polish equivalent of KGB and STASI, but I couldn't care less. I never had any direct contact with the „spooks" and it was the world that for me did not exist, at least for the time being. It was common knowledge that SB had a vast number of „secret collaborators" (or TW's), i.e. informers who snitched on their family, friends, neighbors, and professional colleagues. This network of internal spies was probably never as developed as in the neighboring East Germany, but people were certainly always aware of the fact that anything they said to anyone could land on some aspiring bureaucrat's desk. The standard joke was that whoever didn't drink vodka at a party was probably an informer.

I greeted Sue and her friend Donna in my town and eagerly played a role of an unofficial tour guide, showing them around, pointing out interesting things, and freely exchanging views on all kinds of subjects, including those which were generally „not allowed" in PRL. While Donna was a somewhat weird person, Sue struck me as a much more restrained, thoughtful, and interesting individual. I imagined that I could easily become friends with her, but it was a moot point, because at the end of their second day in Wrocław I took them both to the main railroad station and put them on a train to Cracow. I was absolutely sure I would not see either of them again. But I was wrong.

Contrary to many popular beliefs, travel to countries outside of the communist bloc was possible for average people, especially for citizens of Poland and Hungary where communist stranglehold on the society was least oppressive. While people in the West routinely viewed the Eastern Bloc as a uniform „red" sea, it never was. The most restrictive countries, outside of the Soviet Union, were East Germany, Romania, and Bulgaria.

This is not to say that going to the West from Poland was easy. Just getting all the required paperwork was difficult, and at virtually any moment the authorities could simply bar someone from leaving without giving any reasons for such decisions. People living in PRL didn't have their passports stashed away in drawers at home. Each time someone wanted to travel to the West he or she had to apply for the passport, and such applications were routinely denied. Additionally, private trips were only possible if the interested party had a formal invitation, stamped by a Polish embassy or consulate, from a permanent resident of the destination country. The inviting person basically declared that he or she was taking full financial and legal responsibility for the invitee for the duration of the trip.

What all of that meant in practical terms was that very few people in Poland could deal with all of these obstacles. First of all, nobody knew anybody in the West unless they had some close family abroad. Secondly, even if someone happened to have an acquaintance on the other side of the Iron Curtain, asking such people for a formal invitation to visit them was a tall order.

It was exactly the situation I found himself in. I really wanted to visit England - not to emigrate from Poland for good, but to see with my own eyes the country I learned so much about and to experience firsthand an English-speaking environment. So at the end of 1973 I decided to do the unthinkable - I wrote a letter to Sue asking her for an invitation. It was obviously a very long shot since I didn't really know this person, and she had no idea who I was. To invite someone almost completely unknown for a visit from the communist bloc was a very risky proposition. And yet Sue decided to take that risk. In early 1974 I got the invitation on the basis of which I applied for the passport which I got. Then I went to the British embassy in Warsaw to apply for a visa. This was also successful. Suddenly and unexpectedly the West was within reach.

In the summer of 1975 I boarded a train in Poznań which took me via East and West Germany to the Dutch ferry port of Hoek van Holland. Once there, I boarded a ship which after 5 hours of sailing got me to the English port of Harwich. After just a couple of more hours on the train I arrived at Liverpool Street railway station in London.

The train trip from Poland to Holland contained one stage which was undoubtedly the crowning achievement of the grotesque idiocy dominating the communist world. As the trained entered East Berlin, it stopped at Berlin Ostbahnhof station where soldiers of the GDR border services boarded it and the inspection began while travel continued to the next station called Friedrichstrasse, the last one before West Berlin. There the entire train was surrounded by armed soldiers. Tracking dogs ran under the train carriages while the soldiers boarded again and searched all the possible nooks and crannies. Travelers were no longer allowed to leave their compartments. The walls of the toilets were dismantled, and the covers from the ceilings in the corridors and vestibules were removed. All this in order to search for possible escapees.

After the inspection, all the border guards got off the train, and then something extraordinarily stupid occurred. The East German engine was unhooked and moved to the back of the train. It then pushed all the carriages just up to the border line, at which point it stopped, letting the train roll freely to the western side where it was literally caught by West Berlin railroad workers who made sure that it rolled safely into the Berlin Zoo station, the first one in West Berlin. The astounding thing was that the passengers didn't have to pay for watching this circus. This was the first and last time I saw this spectacle which was one of the saddest symbols of divided Europe. And all of this was done just to prevent the East German train crew from escaping from their "paradise" to the West.

When I got to London, I had exactly 20 dollars in my pocket which was the amount of hard currency the Polish overlords allowed people traveling to the West to legally obtain. This was their peculiar way of saying „You want to travel there? See if you can survive". But I couldn't care less about this financial predicament. I spent some of my dollars on a London Underground ticket to Warwick Station, just a short walk from Sue's apartment which at that time she shared with her partner Hedy.

As I emerged from this station, I saw for the first time in my life just a normal London street, bustling with people and cars, shops enticing clientele with decorative storefronts, and everyday life oozing all kinds of smells and sounds which were alien to a visitor from „the other side". This was indeed a different world in which - I was sure - nothing was rationed, especially female knickers, and in which no one stood in long lines for anything. But the abundance of goods in all the shops, however shocking at first, wasn't that important to me. I suddenly found myself in a free, democratic, English-speaking country, and I could see for myself how dramatically different the lives of average Britons were from my own and my compatriots.

Walking out of that tube station in the summer of 1975 was not about a mundane trip to a foreign country. It was a transformative experience which I would never forget. It is difficult to explain the feelings associated with my emerging onto Warwick Avenue in northwest London. For lack of a better description, it was a sense of exhilarating release from years of debilitating serfdom and mindless propaganda. I found myself in the middle of a vibrant, free European city, and it was just difficult to comprehend what I was experiencing. I knew very well that all of this was temporary, but at that particular moment it didn't matter one bit. It is safe to assume that not a single person living in the vicinity of the Warwick Avenue tube station at that time realized how important their neighborhood briefly became for one citizen of the communist bloc.

I spent countless hours talking to Sue and Hedy, went to see all the „touristy" places in the British capital, met a lot of interesting people, and sampled a bunch of exotic foods, especially Indian curries. The cocoon of 22 years of communist propaganda was beginning to crumble very quickly. For me it was astonishing to see all the newsstands packed with newspapers and magazines offering views on every possible subject in the world. The Hyde Park Corner speakers shouted their opinions to small groups of listeners, and while it was mostly silly, the point was that they could do that without any fear or any censorship.

Westerners in situations like this tend to think a bit simplistically that someone who just got out of the communist world would immediately celebrate his or her freedom and emigrate for good. To some extent that might be true in the case of people relentlessly persecuted, imprisoned, perhaps even tortured. However, in most cases a decision to leave your own country and start a new life somewhere else is never that simple. There are always family and professional considerations, not to mention all kinds of financial ramifications. There is also the fact that emigration is a major shock to someone's existence, regardless of what kind of life this person had previously experienced.

My summer visit to London was never about leaving Poland. It was a fascinating adventure set in a totally new reality. After a few weeks spent with Sue and Hedy, I dutifully boarded the same train going back home. And yet something changed forever. The miracle of Sue and her invitation was that the West ceased to be some distant and unreachable world, full of „imperialists", „ruthless capitalists", and „reactionaries". In time this turned out to be a far-reaching development.

A guy walks down the street carrying a TV set.

„What? Is it broken?" - asks him someone.

„No, I am taking it to church"

„Why?"

„Well, it constantly lies, so it's time for a confession"

Postcard no. 7 - Forbidden thoughts, forbidden words

My gradual transition from being a vassal of a totalitarian state to a person of at least some intellectual freedom began half way through my high school years and continued unabated for the next 15 years. Once this process started, there was no going back, although initially I myself wasn't completely aware of what was happening. By mid-seventies my English was more or less native-like. I spoke with impeccable, southeastern accent, known in linguistic circles as Received Pronunciation, and could easily pass for someone born and raised in England. This ability, which I later lost due to all kinds of linguistic influences (yes, I am talking about you, Americans), was rare in people learning a second language, and it was to become a major problem.

As early as 1973 I began dabbling in journalism which in the communist paradise was a pretty tricky endeavor. Every printed or publicly uttered text, be it in newspapers or on theater stages or in cinemas, had to be perused by state censors who were predominantly stupid bureaucrats making their decisions on the basis of censorship rules constructed by the authorities. There were no uncensored media in PRL, with the exception of a few underground publications which had extremely limited reach.

In my case, I became a freelance writer for a daily called „Gazeta Robotnicza" („Workers' Gazette") which was the local „organ" of the communist party. This was somewhat odd, because at that time I already knew that I didn't want to have anything to do with the state and its idiot guardians, but there were very limited options for people who wanted to pursue journalism. I met a bunch of interesting people working for the same newspaper and became close friends with two of them - Krzysztof and Andrzej. I remained friends with them until they both passed away nearly half a century later.

Writing for this publication was a constant juggling act. Journalists almost automatically used a mechanism of self-censorship. They knew very well what could be published and what was out of the allowed bounds. Additionally, it was generally understood that all the journalists should be members of the communist party. However, I and my friend Krzysztof never signed up for PZPR membership and were the only members of the entire staff who had that dubious status.

This was an unusual situation which resulted in an yearly ritual of being called to the editor-in-chief's office for a peculiar pep-talk. The boss was an intelligent and non-confrontational guy, but he was also a high-ranking party official who had to toe the line. He would sit me in front of his desk and ask: „So, isn't it time for you to join the ranks of PZPR? It would be much better for your career if you did". To which I invariably responded: „Well, I understand, but I am still considering this, and I haven't made any decision yet".

It continued like that for a couple of years. I kept writing my articles, carefully navigating censorship issues, but never engaging in government propaganda. I never wrote a word about „enormous successes" of the socialist economy, nor did I comment on the glorious leaders of the party. On the other hand, the censors never rested - they scanned basically everything for any traces of „ideological impropriety".

My colleagues at the newspaper were a diverse group which mimicked to a large extent various sharp divisions present in the Polish society. Some of them were staunch ideologues, following blindly "the party line" and actually supporting the idea that what people wrote or said in public needed to be strictly controlled, because only then the state could be properly protected from various shady characters. Basically they supported the totalitarian nature of the government. Some other journalists were in the middle - they would never dare to openly challenge the authorities, but privately hated the realities of People's Republic of Poland.

And then there were people like Andrzej, Krzysztof, Tadeusz, and I who thought that we lived in a ridiculous, made up reality, dictated to us by people who were never legally elected to represent anybody and who created a constitutionally illegitimate state called PRL.

These divisions were present everywhere and ran within families. Unfortunately sometimes that resulted in heated arguments spoiling Christmas dinners. It would simply not be true to say that in the 70s and 80s most Poles opposed their communist rulers. Reliable statistics were never available, but it would be safe to assume that a sizable percentage of the population, especially seniors, tolerated the government and supported the idea of leading relatively stable, if not prosperous lives, where lots of things were guaranteed and free, such as health care, pensions or college education.

It was therefore possible to participate in social gatherings during which participants would have major differences of opinion, and tempers would frequently fly. Someone might for example say that there was no real censorship in Poland, because banning stuff was simply a justified defense mechanism, but such a view would be immediately and often ruthlessly countered by people who thought that the country was an authoritarian cesspool. Under such circumstances it was at times pretty difficult to talk rationally to your own family over dinner. Generally speaking, I tried to avoid such conflicts, because they were totally futile.

One day I got a peculiar letter from the Wrocław customs office informing me that I received a book from the United States which „could not be released" because of its „harmful content". The book in question was „1984" by George Orwell which - indeed - featured prominently on the government's no-no list. However, the letter also stated that the addressee had the right to appear in front of a customs officer to appeal this decision. It was odd, because I had no idea that citizens could protest the confiscations of books. Usually the banned stuff was never delivered and that was it. So, I decided to go and see what happens.

And what happened was very strange. The bureaucrat at

the customs office looked at my letter, checked my identity card and asked:

„Did you know that this book was coming?".

„No, I had no idea".

„So why do you need this anticommunist propaganda?"

„I don't need it, but I am at the English Department of the university, so access to such materials is at times useful".

„Wait, do you mean this book is in English?"

„Yes. You didn't look at it?"

„No, I was just given a list. Wait a second".

The guy disappeared and then he came back with the book in hand. He glanced through it, and it was obvious he didn't know a word of English. Then without any explanation or further argument he stamped some paper, handed the book to me and said „Get out of here". He didn't have to say it twice. Apparently once again the government decided that most of the totally stupid masses would never be able to read Orwell in English.

On another occasion I actually got to know the official censor for the city of Jelenia Góra. She was a woman in her early forties who seemed to be hell-bent on dragging my friend Krzysztof to her bed. During a few meetings with her she betrayed no knowledge of anything in particular, and when asked how she made her censorship decisions, she admitted that she usually used a thick book provided by the government with all the rules, prescriptions, and regulations. It was scary to think that artists, journalists, and scientists were being controlled by assholes following blindly governmental dictates.

Actually, I once met a real censorship asshole. In my job as a journalist I sometimes had to deliver in person the latest articles to the printing office. I quickly learned that there was a room in that facility where a morose individual sat all day, read every word to be printed, and sometimes objected to a word, a line, or an entire article. In fact, he had the power to stop the publication of the whole newspaper if he so wished. One day I had to go to his room to ask why he crossed out the word "abrupt" from the sentence "British prime minister

Harold Wilson abruptly resigned". The censor looked at me and simply said: "This is none of your business."

"OK, but what's wrong with abrupt?"

"We cannot say he resigned abruptly, because it implies a crisis or something."

"But it **was** abrupt. What do you want us to say? That he resigned slowly? Or methodically?"

"Doesn't matter. Just say that he resigned."

"And why do we care about how a British leader resigned?"

"Again, it's none of your business."

In 1977 a censor of the name Tomasz Strzyżewski fled Poland to Sweden and took with him hundreds of pages containing the rules of controlling media which he eventually published in London under the title „Black Book of Censorship". Most citizens of Poland, including myself, knew nothing about it back then. Now it is known that this volume contained totally asinine restrictions on even the most trivial subjects. Apparently the rulers didn't want any public discussions of natural or man-made disasters, harmfulness of asbestos, toxicity of plastic Christmas tree decorations or statistics concerning levels of coffee drinking in Poland. Curiously the same ban was not applicable to the data on vodka drinking. There were also arcane rules concerning taking and publishing pictures of the highest ranking state officials who obviously always had to look their best. Since this was before the time of Photoshop and digital photography, recording a „proper" image of a particular ruler sometimes took hours and a lot of wasted film.

Media censorship wasn't the only way of controlling the flow of information in Poland. In my role of a journalist I once visited the main post office building in Wrocław. As I was talking to one of the officials, a door suddenly opened to my right, probably accidentally. I saw, just for a fleeting moment, a room with a very long table at which there was a row of people engaged in the process of steaming letters open. The state needed to know what the hell people wrote to each other, especially to or from foreigners. Just a few weeks later I got a Christmas card from my friend Peter in Scotland who wrote „Best holiday wishes for you and all our readers". No additional comment was necessary.

Censorship sometimes applied to entire buildings. In early 60. it was decided that Wrocław would be the place to display a huge, 19th century painting titled "Panorama Racławicka" ("Racławice Panorama"). It was a canvas more than 100 meters long, depicting the Battle of Racławice in 1794 during which the Polish forces under the command of Tadeusz Kościuszko, the same Kościuszko who earlier had fought in the American war of independence, beat the living daylights out of Russian tsarist army.

The painting was first shown to the public at the end of 19th century in the city of Lwów, but during WWII it was rolled up and hidden away from both the Nazis and the Soviets. After the war it arrived in Wrocław in 1946 where it was first stored in a railroad warehouse, and then in the National Museum cellar. Showing it to the public was not possible unless a dedicated, rotunda-style building was erected, and a decision to build such a structure was made in 1962. But having a building to show the painting was not the only problem.

The construction dragged on forever while the authorities kept deliberating the pros and cons of displaying a work of art which showed a Russian defeat at the hands of the Poles. Ultimately in the 70. the entire project was abandoned, presumably under the pressure from the "brotherly" Moscow comrades. This created a very peculiar situation.

The actual, forsaken rotunda structure was right there, in the center of Wrocław, visible to everyone. And yet nobody was allowed to talk about it or mention in public what it was for. People were supposed to pretend that the building actually didn't exist. It was surrounded by a high fence and left to rot. For years it was never mentioned in any media reports or publications - it was "erased" from public consciousness, very much like Stalin erased people for encyclopedias and historical texts. Apparently, in the convoluted reality of PRL it was possible to rub out not only words, ideas, and thoughts, but also physical buildings made of concrete and steel.

In the few years of my work as a journalist in Wrocław I never even once heard "Panorama Racławicka" being mentioned in any context. That briefly changed in 1979 for reasons to be explained soon.

Why do Polish militia patrols always have
 three guys?

One can read, one can write,
and the third one keeps an eye
on the two intellectuals.

Postcard no. 8 - *Exitus vetitum*

After my return from London I started working on my MA dissertation. Sadly, I was just about to collide with the full force of autocracy. In 1976 a cultural exchange organization in London offered me a very rare chance - I could go to the UK to work for a year in an English high school as a Russian teacher. Obviously this would require permissions from both the university and the government. There was no problem with the former - the dean of my department immediately supported the idea, stressing that living in an English-speaking country for 12 months would be very beneficial to any student of linguistics. The government had a different opinion.

One morning I got a call from a person who introduced himself as Zygmunt (who for simplicity will be called Ziggy) and who said he represented the authorities responsible for either allowing or not allowing my trip to England. I was invited to an interview in the ex-Gestapo red brick building in the center of Wrocław. It was immediately obvious that Ziggy worked for the SB, i.e. the secret police.

One could refuse such an invitation and it was also likely that such a refusal would not immediately result in an extended session of water boarding. However, I really needed to know where I stood with my prospective temporary career of a Russian teacher, so I agreed. What happened then was my first real, direct encounter with the sheer power and abject stupidity of the people who were in charge. When I arrived for my „interview", I was led into a small room with a table and a couple of chairs. No other frills and decorations - just a naked, shabby, repulsive interior.

After a while I was joined by three somber looking individuals who were in no mood for exchanging pleasantries. The conversation went like this.

„So you know who we are, right?"

„Yes, I think so."

„OK. We understand that you want to go to the UK for a year to work at a school".

„Yes."

„Why?"

"It's a great opportunity to improve my English and gain teaching skills."

"But you are supposed to teach Russian."

"Yes, but in an English speaking country."

"Do you know which school you would be going to?"

"No, it will be assigned once I am there."

"How do you know it's just a job offer?"

"What do you mean?"

"They may try to get information from you or coerce into something."

"Well, I really don't have any information. And who do you mean by they?"

"Never mind that. We might give you a passport if you would help us a bit."

"In what way?"

"Well, on your return we would like you to write a detailed report containing accounts of all your contacts, meetings, conversations, etc."

"So, you would like me to spy on people."

"No, it's not really spying. Just sharing information."

"I don't think I can agree to do that."

"Are you sure? You know, your life could become much easier if you decide to cooperate. And if you decide otherwise, there may be some negative consequences. We are talking about future job prospects, getting your own apartment, and traveling abroad. You don't have to give us your answer right now. Just think about it for a while and let us know".

At no point during this strange interview was there any danger of violence and no direct threats were uttered. And yet I felt totally violated by this dark, governmental force. I thought about it and let them know - the answer was still "no". A few days later I got a letter informing me that my application for a passport had been denied. No reason given - the rulers didn't have to explain their decisions to anybody.

This was the first time that I was expressly barred from leaving my own country. Of course I knew about all the rules and regulations, but previously none of this stuff ever applied to me. Now it did, and it generated lots of questions, the most important one being: why was it necessary to restrict a simple right to travel abroad?

In fact what happened to me was relatively routine. SB frequently barred people from traveling abroad to force them into cooperation. In the 70. there was a very well-known Polish journalist, novelist and poet, Ryszard Kapuściński, who traveled the world at will and was once considered a serious contender for Nobel Prize in literature. In 2007, shortly after his death, it turned out that he was working with SB from 1965 to 1977. His wife Alicja defended him by saying that all Polish journalists traveling to the West were automatically regarded as "potential informers" by SB. That may be true, but it was probably also true that Kapuściński's cooperation had to be voluntary and not just potential, because otherwise he wouldn't be able to travel all around the globe whenever he wanted.

For SB restricting freedom of travel was a very powerful tool which they used quite often, mainly in the form of simple blackmail: "yes, you can go to Greece, Spain, or France, but only if you decide to help us with X, Y or Z". The only people relatively free to travel without conditions were party leaders, famous sport personalities, and well-known scientists. It is impossible to say how many people decided to be SB informants just because they wanted to visit someone in the West. But it is certain that a lot of them left, and never returned.

Seemingly stuck in Poland for a while, I observed the usual farce of "parliamentary elections". By that time I knew very well that the voters didn't really elect anybody, because the winners were predetermined by PZPR. There was an organization called Front Jedności Narodu (National Unity Front) which was responsible for periodically organizing the sham spectacle and produced lists of candidates in all the electoral districts. Nobody really knew by what methodology and by whom people were selected to be candidates, but it didn't matter.

The way that this ridiculous system worked was that people in the first two spots on the ballot were practically guaranteed to win, because - in order for them to lose - over 99% of the voters would have to cross their names out. In practice almost nobody crossed out anything, because everybody knew it was totally pointless. On the election Sunday people trudged to the polling stations like mindless lemmings, and dropped their untouched ballots into the box, thus fulfilling their "civic duty". The following morning it was usually announced that 99% of the voters had showed up to cast their ballots. It was surprising that they never announced that 105% of all the voters had participated in the election.

In Stalinist times there was a predominant if unsubstantiated view that not voting could be punished in some way by the authorities. This explained why my father insisted that I go and vote when I turned 18. And so, I did. Having crossed all the names out, I put the ballot in the box and left. I never took part in this pitiful parody again.

Yet the communists kept saying with straight faces that Poland had free and fair elections. Invariably on Monday after the election TV news showed some 95-year old "babcia" (grandmother) who had come to the polling station at 6 am to be first in line to cast her meaningless vote. She was usually given a bouquet of flowers by the grateful authorities. All of this was blatantly stupid, staged, and laughable, but people went through the prescribed motions, because it was "the thing to do".

An American meets a Russian.
"I have 3 cars" - says the American.
"I use one to go to work, the other one to go shopping, and the third one to visit neighbors"
"I have two cars" - responds the Russian.
"I use one for work, and the other one for shopping"
"How do you visit your neighbors?"
"I use tanks for that"

Postcard no. 9 - Colorless green ideas sleep furiously

Given the fact that I wasn't allowed to go to England greatly diminished my chances of going anywhere in the West in the foreseeable future. I did manage to travel two more times to the UK, but these were short, summer trips which apparently Ziggy and his buddies regarded as harmless student escapades.

But I didn't give up. While finishing my dissertation, I maintained numerous contacts with westerners: Sue, Peter, Jean and a number of Britons or Americans who either worked temporarily in Wrocław or were just passing through. These were usually either teachers, journalists or students.

One such person was a young, aspiring theater director, Travis, whom I met at a "Polish summer camp" the purpose of which was unclear. In large measure it was probably a propaganda stint by the PRL government, trying to show a bunch of "Yankees" the dubious glory of the "people's republic".

One day Travis suggested that I should write to an American authority in my chosen field and ask him or her about the possibility of studying in the US for a semester or two while finishing my dissertation. This was an oddly interesting idea, although the chances of success were pretty remote. I knew exactly who to write to.

At that time professor Noam Chomsky, the head of the Department of Linguistics at M.I.T., was a world-renowned scholar and a leading proponent of his own theory of language which centered on the idea of the so-called universal grammar, i.e. a purported common, underlying structure of all human languages. In linguistic and philosophical circles he was a towering persona. He was also a political activist whose views were radically leftist, at least in the context of public discourse in America. For example, he was a staunch opponent of the Vietnam war and often criticized the so-called American imperialism which earned him a spot on Richard Nixon's "enemies list".

Chomsky's linguistic books were full of examples that since then have become classics. He used the sentence "Colorless green ideas sleep furiously" to illustrate the fact that an utterance in English (or any other language) can be grammatically perfect, and yet semantically absurd. And he always asked his students to tell him why the sentence "Flying planes can be dangerous" was ambiguous.

Chomsky became the addressee of my letter. It was a short text in which I explained my interest in his linguistic theories and briefly discussed the subject matter of my dissertation titled "Child Language Acquisition" which had some Chomskian undertones. The letter was obviously a rather desperate shot in the dark, and no response was ever expected. But a response did come. Chomsky himself wrote back, inviting me to come to M.I.T. and offering free studies for two semesters.

This was a shocking development. The letter in itself didn't guarantee anything, because it wasn't a formal invitation. However, I showed it to both the dean of my department and my Scottish teacher Peter. Both of them immediately said they would support my trip to the US. Unfortunately, I needed more than their support. So, once again, I submitted an application for an „exit visa", i.e. a passport. Ziggy and his crew reacted almost immediately, asking me to attend another interview. However, this time around I had a secret plan. I decided that I would agree to writing a report after my return from America, except for the fact that I would not return immediately. I would go from the US to London and accept the Russian teacher job offer which was still open. In other words, I planned to do what I was not allowed to do earlier.

Additionally I decided that while in America I would apply

to some US colleges to see if I could get accepted into PhD programs. I thought it would be a good test of my future chances of studying abroad, and doing this while in America was much easier than it would be when in Poland.

This time Ziggy had no problem with my trip to the US, because he was an idiot and had no idea about what was going on. However, there was another obstacle. I had to go to the American consulate in Poznań to apply for an entry visa in person. This was a pretty surreal experience worthy of a Monty Python sketch. The consulate was guarded by a uniformed US Marine soldier whose countenance was such that being shot by him for no apparent reason was certainly a possibility. After all, he was guarding a small piece of American territory in the middle of communist Poland. I was a part of that Poland, so potentially I was an enemy. These were painful realities of the Cold War, and nobody could do anything about it. The soldier asked me why I wanted to enter the consulate, and then let me in through a narrow corridor to the office where two women were sitting at their desks behind glass screens. I came up to one of them, gave her my visa application and was told to sit and wait. I did, but not for long. Very soon the same woman emerged from the consular innards to tell me that the visa application was denied.

"Why?" - I asked.

"I am sorry, sir, but we are not at liberty to say."

"Really? So what is my next step?"

"Well, you can try some other time. Like in a year or two."

I was not ready to quit. I had a unique, once in a lifetime opportunity to not only go to the US, but also meet and study with arguably the most important figure in my field, at least at that time.

"Can I speak to the consul?" - I asked.

"Technically you can."

"What do you mean by that?"

"You can certainly ask to see the consul, but you probably won't."

"Do you decide that?"

"Yes."

"OK then, I request to see the consul".

"Fine. Your request is denied."

At this point it was obvious that the chances of actually talking to the consul face to face were none. However, there was a middle-aged man, hovering in the background and listening to my conversation, who suddenly came up to the woman at the desk and whispered something in her ear. This had a surprising effect. The woman told me to wait for a few minutes and then invited me to the consul's office. Soon enough I was sitting in front of a relatively young man who asked a simple question.

"So why do you want to go to the US?".

I could say all kinds of things. Instead I shoved my letter from Noam Chomsky in front of his face and explained that I got a unique invitation from a world-famous scholar to come to M.I.T. for purely academic purposes. I also added that I had no intention of staying in the US past my allotted time. The consul read the letter, paused for a while, and then without a word took my passport to stamp an American visa in it. "Have a good trip" - he said.

In 1977 I boarded a rickety, Russian-made jet called Ilyushin-62, lovingly known as "the flying coffin", and departed Warsaw for JFK. In New York I was met by a friend of mine who drove me to Boston and hosted me in a rented house full of college students, some of whom were pretty weird. Almost everybody in this environment smoked pot. People came in and out, and some of them stayed overnight with their "partners". It was a pretty chaotic scene. My friend, whom I met a year earlier in Poland and who came from a rich Jewish family in Maryland, seemed to have some romantic designs on me (or so I recklessly thought at the time), but I was not interested. What I was really interested in was my stint at one of the top colleges in America.

On a memorable day in the summer of 1977 I walked into one of the buildings on the M.I.T. campus where I had an appointment with Chomsky. After a brief wait I was led into his office and sat in front of him across a rather messy desk. This was an astounding event in my relatively short life. I was a nobody from a communist country facing a famous linguist. Noam was very friendly, asked a couple of questions and assured me that I could participate in any lectures or seminars I wanted. We engaged in a brief conversation about trivialities.

The meeting was fascinating, but it also had a perplexing background. Chomsky knew that I was from Poland, but never said a word about politics. Neither did I, but I suspected that my host's views on communism, Soviet Union, Cold War and many other issues were much more leftist than mine. It was a strange paradox. This famous scientist favored a lot of ideas that I had been assiduously shedding. In fact, it was difficult for me to understand why someone like Chomsky might harbor such sentiments. I assumed, probably correctly, that it was easy for an inhabitant of the free world to espouse virtually any views since doing so had no practical consequences and entailed no dangers. On the other hand, Chomsky was certainly not an opportunist.

All of that, however, was not important. The next months were filled with intriguing lectures, wonderful discussions about linguistics, walking trips around Boston, and informal conversations with Chomsky as well as other professors and fellow students. My friend was not a particularly helpful host, perhaps because our relationship did not progress far enough, but I couldn't complain, because she was helping me survive in America. She also insisted on driving me all the way to Baltimore to visit her parents.

It was a pretty strange visit. Her parents, while friendly and hospitable, made a point of showing me various memorabilia and photo albums, some of which referred to "difficult" episodes in Polish-Jewish relations. These have always been very complicated issues, and it was difficult to react to this in any polite and rational way, so I basically didn't. Moreover, at this stage of my life I wasn't really too much interested in any of this. I breathed and experienced America all around me, enjoying every minute of it.

It was then that I made an irrevocable decision - I was going to emigrate from Poland for good, although not before settling the matter of my degree from Wrocław University. I no longer wanted to be a citizen of communist Europe and I came to the conclusion, actually shared by many historians, that the abolition of the post-war division of Europe would require another world war. I wasn't prepared to wait for a miracle that might never come. My mind's transition was complete, although the road to emigration was as complicated as ever.

As I promised myself, I filed applications for graduate studies at five different colleges: two in Canada, and three in the US, including some prestigious ones, like Brown and Cornell. There was no way of telling whether anything would come out of that, but I treated these applications as an experiment which was almost doomed to failure.

When my stay in the US was coming to a close, I sold my prized possession, an East German SLR camera, Praktica, and bought a ticket to London. I landed at Heathrow clutching a valuable item - my completed MA dissertation annotated by Noam Chomsky.

A communist is a person who read all the works of Marx, Engels, and Lenin.

An anticommunist is the same person who read all of this, and understood it.

Postcard no. 10 - In the shadow of Thomas Becket

 I had a joyous reunion with Sue and her friends, loitered a bit in London for a few months, and then reported to the organization offering me a year-long contract to teach Russian. I learned that I was assigned to go to Simon Langton Grammar School for Boys in Canterbury. The school was a private institution located just outside of a beautiful ancient town in Kent, where the entire landscape was dominated by a magnificent cathedral - the seat of the Anglican Church.

Back in the year 1170 the archbishop of Canterbury, Thomas Becket, was brutally murdered inside this church. Both the cathedral and the town center surrounding it were utterly enchanting and I couldn't be happier to land a job in such a glorious place. I became a member of the school staff, albeit only temporarily, interacted with my colleagues and students, and became friends with two young female language teachers from Germany and Spain. For the first time in my life I was almost a part of free society, with many international contacts, access to virtually any information, and freedom to do whatever I wanted.

My stay in Britain was not without some challenges. A few older teachers were weary of having a colleague from Eastern Europe, and were even suggesting that teaching Russian to young Britons was potentially a dangerous attempt at communist infiltration. The divide between East and West was present even in an English high school which to me was both surprising and sad.

On weekends I would almost always hop on a train to go to London where I met with Sue and her new partner (future husband) Louis. The three of us did pub crawls, went for walks, sampled all kinds of restaurants, and spent evenings talking about virtually any subject under the sun. These were wonderful times and for me it was my introduction to everyday life in the West. Louis turned out to be a very friendly, jovial character which was a blessing, because to some extent my stay in Canterbury was an exercise in loneliness.

Before I showed up in Canterbury, the company that arranged my stint as a Russian teacher offered me a quick, 10-day summer job. I was supposed to be a guide and translator for a group of about 20 Soviet teachers from the city of Chelyabinsk. I accepted the offer, and this job turned out to be a very peculiar experience. The teachers were all relatively young, mostly in their thirties, and none of them had ever left the Soviet Union before. Also, none of them spoke any English whatsoever. On top of that, although they came from a large Russian city, Chelyabinsk, it is a place that sits at the foot of the Ural Mountains, at the border of Europe and Asia, and is relatively isolated from the the rest of the world.

I met this group at a London office of an organization that was involved in Anglo-Soviet exchange programs. The Russians were a friendly and boisterous bunch, with the exception of their KGB minder who pretended to be a teacher as well, but who was a dour jackass whose job was to make sure that the people under his watch did not try to escape or make too much contact with the Anglo-Saxon populace at large. However, initially the biggest problem arose when I introduced myself to the group and told the Russians that I was a Polish national staying and working temporarily in the UK. This was totally incomprehensible to them. They did not understand how a citizen of the communist world could possibly travel individually to the West and work there.

Once they chewed on this information for a while, I was generally accepted as the group's guide and interpreter. This was greatly helped by the fact that we travelled to various places in the UK, like Oxford, and we stayed at hotels where every single evening a delegate of the Russian group would knock on my door and would say the following: *Приглашаем вас на вечеринку*. This translates as "we invite you to a soiree", but what it actually meant was that we all gathered in a single hotel room and the Russians produced endless bottles of vodka which we consumed in vast quantities as warm straight shots. After a few sessions like that we could have easily renegotiated the postwar division of Europe or the Arab-Israeli conflict, but we never bothered.

One day during this journey we visited the Windsor Castle. After the official tour the Soviet visitors were attracted by a music store which was right outside the gates of the royal abode. They all went in, and they all emerged out of there with exactly same album in their hands: "Hotel California" by The Eagles. I couldn't help thinking that they behaved very much like their totalitarian country expected them to do - uniformly. They spent their few moments of freedom in the West on buying the same thing, as if ordered to do so, although I doubt Brezhnev was ever an Eagles fan.

One evening, after dinner in a hotel restaurant, I sat alone with a woman called Daria. We were sipping drinks and chatting in Russian about everything and nothing. She must have been about 10 years older than me, and she told be that back home she taught chemistry. During this conversation she asked me what my dreams for the future were. I told her, truthfully, that I wanted to leave Poland for good and start a new life in the West. She was shocked and asked me why. It became obvious to me very quickly that I couldn't rationally explain to her my decision to emigrate. In a strange way, we already belonged to two dramatically different worlds. She was still a captive of the communist world, and I wasn't, although technically I was still stuck on the wrong side of the Iron Curtain.

After about six months I got responses from American colleges. All of them accepted me to their graduate schools, however only one, University of Illinois, offered not only tuition cost coverage, but also a teaching assistantship which would guarantee a small monthly income. Obviously I had no money, so I quickly decided that the best option was to go to Chicago. I wrote the school a letter accepting their offer and after a few weeks got official paperwork which was needed to get a US student visa known as F-1.

I was now facing a major dilemma. The MA dissertation was done, but I didn't complete the process of getting my degree back in Poland. I could therefore go back to my country and finish that, hoping that Ziggy and his jerks would allow me to leave again for US studies. Or I could simply fly back to America, start my doctorate courses, and then apply for permanent US immigrant visa. I chose the latter which meant that potentially my exodus from Poland could have happened in 1978 or early 1979. It didn't, courtesy of US immigration law.

With university acceptance papers in hand, I showed up at the US embassy in London to apply for a student visa. I was almost immediately informed that such a visa could not be issued. Here is the conversation with the US embassy employee:

„We cannot grant you this visa while you are in Great Britain."

„What?"

„In order to get a student visa, you have to apply for it in your own country."

„Sir, do you understand that if I go back to my country, I may never be able to apply for anything?"

"Well, I am sorry, but this doesn't matter. We have these rules and we have to follow them."

„Are there any exceptions to these rules?"

„Yes, but only in very special cases."

„Like what?"

„Again, it doesn't matter. Your case doesn't qualify. Please go back to Poland and apply there".

And that is what I did. Having said goodbye to my school, my colleagues, Sue, Louis, and a bunch of other people, I boarded a train which took me first to London, then to Harwich, then to Hoek van Holland, and then once again to People's Republic of Poland. I was back where I started, but there were two substantial changes. First, I knew I wanted to get out of my homeland as soon as possible. Second, I had in my possession acceptance papers from University of Illinois which were valid for a few years. It was a ticket to my potential future.

A Russian comes to Poland under martial law and checks into a hotel. When he tries to make a phone call, he hears a pre-recorded message:
"Conversation monitored, conversation monitored"
"Wow" - he thinks - "What sophistication! They actually tell you upfront you will be snitched on"

UNIWERSYTET
WROCŁAWSKI

DYPLOM

UKOŃCZENIA JEDNOLITYCH
STUDIÓW MAGISTERSKICH

Postcard no. 11 - Lack of distinction

On my return to Poland it was time to get my degree. I submitted the finished MA dissertation and passed the final exam in December of 1978. I was awarded a diploma „with distinction" which was equivalent to what is called *summa cum laude*. However, a few days after this award was given I was called to the office of the head of the English Department, professor Jan Cygan, who was an intellectual giant, and one of the most honest persons I ever got to know. After the war he came to Wrocław from Lwów and actually managed to start and sustain the so-called English Philology, despite the fact that the project was then viewed with utmost suspicion by the authorities.

The conversation between professor Cygan and I was cryptic and definitely worthy of the idiocy that PRL was:

„So, you were awarded a diploma with distinction, but unfortunately this has been taken away."

„Taken away?"

„Yes. You cannot have that, because of some interventions from certain people, or rather organizations."

„I see."

„As you may understand, I cannot do anything about it, so let's just move on."

„Right. I think it is the best option. Thank you for letting me know."

„Yes, thank you. It's a bit awkward for me, but that's the way it has to be. Sorry."

„Understood."

Neither the professor nor I mentioned any particular person or organization, but we both knew what we were talking about. The secret police (SB) had exacted their revenge for my „insubordination", i.e. for my taking up the job in England. It was both a punishment and a warning. The punitive part of this was of no consequence, because I couldn't care less about my distinction or lack thereof, although it was really irritating that an internal spy service had the power to interfere in academic affairs. As for the warning, it was impossible to predict what it would mean, but it got obvious very soon.

I was invited to yet another interview, this time with Ziggy only. It was definitely different than the previous encounters. My interlocutor was much more direct and at times aggressive, but also more open about what exactly SB expected me to do. First, he admitted that the diploma had been stripped of the distinction on orders issued by the police to the university, which was obvious to begin with. Second, he warned me that my life would have many other „negative aspects" if I didn't change my tune and start cooperating. And third, he explained that because of my fluency in English and many contacts with westerners I was in an uniquely good position to keep an eye on foreigners coming to Poland. Basically what Ziggy wanted was someone in Wrocław who could maintain contacts with foreign guests and then report on their activities. Curiously, he also alluded to the fact that in the future I might be allowed to go to the West for work or study, but with specific tasks, for example to get in touch with people SB was interested in.

At that point I actually asked him what role he saw for me while abroad. His answer was both convoluted and bonkers. Basically he said that they (SB) would never send me out of Poland with a specific mission or task, but they would give me names of people I should be trying to become friends with. Alarmingly, he admitted that a lot these people might be members of the Polish community in London, Chicago, and New York. „However, you would never be really working for us" - he added - „It's just collecting information and giving it to us". This was a classic definition of a snitch and right then and there I promised myself that I would never in any way spy on Polish emigre circles. I kept that promise through a lot of pretty turbulent events.

It was obvious that the secret police was trying to coerce me into cooperating with them by screwing up my academic records and threatening unspecified consequences. Little did they know that it was way to late for that. And professor Cygan, who died only recently at a very advanced age, gave me a firm, if nondescript, view of what communist Poland was really like. Although by that time I already had a pretty good idea.

It should be stressed that it was quite possible to live in PRL for decades without ever having anything to do with the people in power, police, secret police, etc. One could lead a pretty mundane life - not very prosperous, but far from the machinery of communist oppression. The trouble started whenever someone wanted to publicly express his or her views, write books, voice „incorrect" opinions, pursue an artistic career or acquire some special skills which would be regarded as useful but potentially dangerous. Otherwise the government left the vast majority of citizens to their own meager resources.

The problem was I came to the conclusion that I would never be left alone. It was obvious that someone in SB had decided that in some fashion I could be useful to them. I doubted it was Ziggy's determination. He was just a vehicle for his superiors, whoever they were. So, at the age of 25 I was faced with a real possibility of being constantly pressured and hounded by people I despised and by forces I didn't want to have anything to do with.

On the other hand, among my friends I did not hide the fact that I had contacts with SB people, so this whole situation didn't weigh heavily on me as a dark secret. In fact, at one point Ziggy asked me to jot down a phone number I should use to contact him, but insisted that I shouldn't write it in the usual way, but as an addition column. If the number was 234-56 (Poland had 5-digit numbers back then), I should write it down as:

$$\begin{array}{r} 23 \\ 45 \\ +\ 6 \\ \hline = 74 \end{array}$$

He must have thought he was being very sneaky and

clever, but when I mentioned this notation during a meeting with a group of friends, one of them burst out laughing, because she also had a number which she was told to write down the same way. It was a great relief to realize that there were other people besides me who had to deal with SB, but unfortunately it seemed unavoidable that I would hear from Ziggy again and again, *ad nauseam*. I wondered however whether SB sometimes asked people to use different methods of phone number notation, such as multiplication, square roots, integrals or differential equations. Perhaps that would require too much mathematical knowledge.

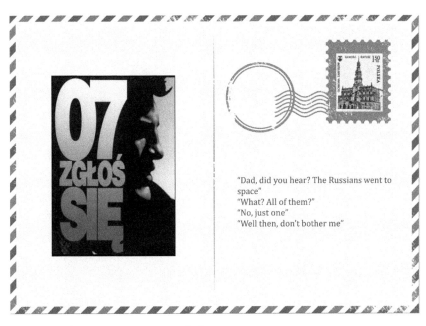

"Dad, did you hear? The Russians went to space"
"What? All of them?"
"No, just one"
"Well then, don't bother me"

Postcard no. 12 - Agent (0)07

Although the meeting with Ziggy once again resulted in no agreement, I felt that the pressure on me had been substantially increased. It was one thing to have an academic degree „devalued" on orders from the spooks, and another to be engaged in secret police activities against foreigners. I sensed that sooner or later there would have to come some kind of major reckoning. My situation would however become much more complicated in very short order.

It was true that I was in touch with many people in the West. Those who actually came to Poland and met me were typically journalists, artists, teachers, and academics. I often served as their interpreter or guide. This obviously entailed traveling with them and spending lots of time on various conversations, most of which were inconsequential. But some were at times a bit intriguing and indicated that a few of these people were in my country on missions to collect information. I never asked them questions about that, nor did I have any proofs of their "unofficial" activities. But it was definitely a bit strange to be asked by a foreigner about a layout of a particular building or about detailed structure of some organization.

And then there were also weird suggestions. In the fall of 1978 I met an Australian reporter who invited me to dinner and, while eating his dessert, asked me a shockingly unusual question:

„Did you ever have contacts with Polish secret police?"

I had absolutely no reason to hide anything, because I never swore to keep my talks with Ziggy secret and never made any commitments. So I told my Australian dinner companion that I had been interviewed a few times by SB agents about my travels to the West. The conversation which followed was both astonishing and disturbing:

„Do you expect to be interviewed by these people in the future?"

„Yes."

„Are you dreading this prospect?"

„Sure, but as you know I live in a country where these things are almost routine".

„Perhaps I can offer a suggestion. Next time they want you to do something for them, agree."

„What?"

„Just agree and see where it will take you".

„I know where it will take me. I will become their informer".

„Not if you inform the people involved that you are going to inform on them."

„So, if I snitch on you, for example, you would need to know about it beforehand".

„Exactly, although I don't give a crap about being snitched on. And while it's all happening, it would be great if you could share with me some information about their methods, questioning tactics, interests, concerns, etc."

„Great. Are you really a reporter?"

„Who gives a shit? It's just a suggestion. Think about it. I am not a spy. Just being nosy. And one more thing - if they ever offer you money, take it and give it to some charity. Otherwise they will become suspicious".

„Are you crazy?"

„No, just practical. Again, think about it".

The Australian introduced himself as Walter. He gave me his phone number in Warsaw and asked me to call whenever there was any need. Whether he was really Walter or really a reporter seemed to be an open and unanswerable question. He never said what publication he worked for and what exactly he was doing in Poland. However, he was probably a real Australian, judging by his heavily accented "aussie" English. He became the first western journalist who openly asked me for information on SB methods of operation. He was also the first to suggest "feeding" Ziggy with false or partially false crap.

The problem was that within just a few months I came into contact with at least 5 other westerners who could be also classified as being excessively nosy and who were also interested in all kinds of information. This was becoming a grotesque situation. People like Ziggy wanted me to spy on foreigners while foreigners wanted me to agree to that, tell them about it, and then spy back.

Nobody at either side of this strange situation ever wanted to recruit me as a full-blown agent, and no proposals were made to that effect. This was understandable, because I had no access to privileged information and held no important positions in the government or anywhere else. But I suddenly found myself in a strange situation where technically I had to choose sides and allegiances. For example, was collecting information on SB for foreign assets an act of betrayal or perhaps even treason? Or was aiding western countries in their efforts to infiltrate communist secret police helping the cause of freedom in Poland?

Ultimately, after a lot of tormented and mostly pointless deliberations, I decided on a potentially risky course of action. I would agree to cooperate with Ziggy and his bunch as much as possible, and gather as much information as possible for friendly Australians, British academics, American journalists, or whatever. I hoped that all of this was a very short-lived arrangement, because my plans to go to University of Illinois were very much on, and my intention to emigrate for good never changed.

However, my decision had one unpleasant consequence. I had to meet with Ziggy on a relatively regular basis, usually once a month. These meetings no longer took place in the ex-Gestapo headquarters, but at an empty apartment in the center of the city. Additionally, whatever I told Ziggy for some reason couldn't be recorded, but had to be hand-written, so both of us sometimes spent a couple of hours in that stupid apartment, while I was busy with my dubious calligraphy.

What I wrote in my horrible handwriting was mostly

absolute bullshit, prearranged with my Western friends. But spending such a long time with Ziggy, who just couldn't keep his fucking mouth shut, gave me a fascinating insight not only into his character, but also into the organization he worked for.

Ziggy was an absolute moron. He claimed he had a law degree, but it was difficult to believe that, based on how he spoke and what he was saying. Sometimes in his chaotic ramblings he would say such idiotic things as „we are especially concerned about British agents who are everywhere", which meant he watched too many James Bond movies which were forbidden in PRL. He lived in an illusory reality of agent 007, full of fast cars, fast women, and vodka martinis, while his own life was probably full of slow cars, zero women, and shots of warm moonshine. His general knowledge of the world was virtually none, and he seemed to be absolutely convinced that he played a vital role in defending Poland from British spies and internal riff-raff. Unfortunately (or fortunately), he was a primitive half-wit who could be easily manipulated or fooled, which I did on a number of occasions.

One time Ziggy asked me about my ex-teacher, Peter, who earlier had left Poland and returned home.

„We are sure he is an MI6 agent" - he said unexpectedly.

„Why do you think that?" - I asked, struggling to hide my merriment.

„I can't go into details, but let me just say that his wife Jean isn't really his wife and she was sent here with him as a cover. Did you ever see anything which would corroborate that?".

„No, not really".

„Did he ever ask you suspicious questions?"

„No" (but an Australian did, you dumbshit, I thought).

It was all monumental idiocy fueled by Ziggy's paranoia about British spies. Of course Peter could be a spy, but if so, his work as a lecturer at the Wrocław University wasn't getting him close to any state secrets. As for Jean, I had absolutely no doubts that she was Peter's wife, but I wondered how SB reached their conclusions. Did they spy on them to count the weekly number of marital fornications? Did they eavesdrop on their conversations? All of that was possible. Peter and Jean lived in an apartment provided by the college, and their place was almost certainly bugged. Anyway, I managed to inform Peter about this conversation via a British friend who was going back to his country. I am sure he immediately told Jean that he had had enough of their false matrimony.

The fact that Ziggy kept asking questions and blabbered crap about his work and his agency's interests gave me a lot of material to share with my western contacts. I told them all about his fixation with British spies, SB's general methodology in dealing with informants, and the intent of questions being asked. In return they gave me information, probably all bogus, which I shared with gleeful Ziggy, who must have thought he was getting valuable intelligence. This charade continued for months. At times it was tiring, but it was also very intriguing.

The Australian was right about one thing. After a few months Ziggy did offer me money. It was a negligible amount, but I accepted it per Walter's advice, and then almost immediately donated it to the Catholic charity organization Caritas which was the only one I knew to be relatively independent of the government. Because I didn't want to show my face at some Caritas office, I sent the donation via a cash money transfer which I signed „Washington Irving", mimicking the actions of my favorite character in the Joseph Heller novel „Catch 22", Yossarian. For the next couple of years I made a few more such donations, always signing the same name. Unfortunately that meant that Caritas was partially funded by the secret police, although on a minuscule scale.

Many years later, when Poland became a free country again, it turned out that Ziggy was the son of a secret service officer who in the first years after the war fought against the so-called „Ukrainian bandits", and was killed by them. So, when in 1971 my interrogator first applied for a job with SB, in his application he wrote that he was raised as an orphan and was taken care of by the security services, so now he wanted to repay his debt to them. What a moving story!

Before he was transferred to Wrocław, Ziggy worked as a local SB chief in a small town of Środa Śląska where apparently he was feared because of his rudeness and threatening behavior. But of course that was well before his personality was presumably tempered by sham law studies and unique focus on chasing English spies. If I could have contacted MI6 back then, I would probably have told them that as far as Wrocław was concerned they had nothing to worry about - the guy in charge of fighting them didn't have adequate skills to tie his shoes successfully or wipe his rear end, even with "Pravda" sheets.

ZOMO riot police stopped a student who was distributing fliers in the street. However, they noticed that sheets of paper were empty.

"Why are you giving out blank sheets of paper?" - they asked.

"Everybody knows what should be written on them" - he responded.

Postcard no. 13 - Lucy in the sky (without diamonds)

.

Despite all the complications arising from the diploma matters and contacts with SB, I was still busy plotting my final exit from Poland. I thought that by the end of 1979 or in the beginning of 1980 I would be in a position to submit my University of Illinois papers and once again ask for US visa. I certainly never expected the complications that arose within just a few months.

Towards the end of 1978 my brother Tomek introduced me to two beautiful young women, Ewa and Lucyna, who were his friends from college. All four of us started getting together, typically over a bunch of drinks and something to eat. These were not gatherings at restaurants, clubs or other venues. Usually we met at Ewa's and Lucyna's rented apartment, which was a tiny basement room with an adjacent bathroom which almost invariably totally froze in winter time.

These were very pleasant meetings, frozen toilet notwithstanding, and as the time went by I started thinking of Lucyna (Lucy) as a possible partner. However, I was very realistic. It was difficult to imagine that someone like Lucy would want to become friends, romantic or otherwise, with a red-haired scraggy looking wimp. And I was right, because for a long time she showed absolutely no interest in me, other than in the context of joint meetings with Ewa and Tomek.

The winter of 1978 was very severe, with extremely low temperatures and heavy snow fall. In December I and my friend were sent to the town of Lubin by our newspaper to do a couple of interviews at the copper mine there. The place was about 40 miles west of Wrocław. It so happened that Lucy lived in this town with her parents, and her father actually worked at the mine. However, I had no intention of suddenly showing up at Lucy's doorstep. We were housed in a hospitality center run by the mine and we had no plans to meet anybody other than the people with whom we had appointments. The weather had other ideas.

Because of a major winter storm, electricity went out on our first night in Lubin. We were cold and hungry, and didn't have things like flashlights or candles. Faced with this dire situation, I told my friend that I actually knew someone in town and that she lived within walking distance from where we were. So we walked and after about 15 minutes we showed up at Lucy's place. She was understandably very surprised, as were her parents. But they gave the two of us flashlights and something to eat. In this strange and unexpected way I got to meet Lucy's parents, and then also her younger sister, Iwona. The next evening, when the lights were back on, Lucy came with Iwona to the hospitality center and we all had a few drinks.

When both Lucy and I got back to Wrocław, our occasional meetings with Ewa and Tomek continued. Sometimes we also went to the movies and parties together. Then my sister Jola and my brother-in-law took us on a day trip to East Berlin where I saw for the first time the shabby looking Berlin Wall over which one could barely see the world I wanted to become a part of. It was all very nice, but none of these events moved the needle as far as my relationship with Lucy was concerned. She was still not interested.

This was more or less confirmed in the summer of 1979 when all of us, together with my newspaper friend Krzysztof and his wife Elżbieta, went on vacation to Bulgaria, via Hungary. These were of course Warsaw Pact countries, so traveling there was relatively easy, because the travelers could only see and hear more or less the same shit as in Poland. Throughout this trip Lucy was kind of distant, not only from me, but from the entire group, which to some extent spoiled everyone's time. It almost felt like she didn't really want to come on this trip in the first place, but joined us, because earlier she had said she would.

Be it as it may, when we all got back home, Lucy went to Lubin and I decided that it was the end of my „Lucy in the Sky with Diamonds" story. Except it wasn't. While the diamonds were definitely out of the picture, the social gatherings of our four continued on and off for months.

Lucy was a weird creature. Sometimes she would almost suggest to me that we could possibly be more then friends, but then she quickly withdrew to her usual posture of almost total indifference. She was both sociable and aloof, fun and moody, interesting and irritating, friendly and reluctant. In some ways I was infatuated with her, but practically gave up on the idea that she could somehow be a major part of my life. Although our acquaintance persisted, it became a series of endless ups and downs leading to nowhere.

There was another factor in all of this which couldn't be ignored. I knew very well that getting involved with any woman at this stage of my life would weigh heavily on my emigration plans. Whether it would be Lucy or someone else, I didn't see how I could suddenly say to this person that what I really wanted was to get the hell out of Poland for good. Therefore the best course of action was definitely staying away from involvements with the opposite sex.

That proved to be difficult. I couldn't deny to myself that I was more and more intrigued with the mystery of the woman from Lubin. However, all of that was abruptly interrupted by events which proved to be enormously important.

"What will happen next?" - asks general Jaruzelski, looking at his portrait hanging on the wall.

"Nothing. They will take me down, and hang you" - answers the picture.

Postcard no. 14 - The three (American) musketeers

101

In late 1979 I got a strange call from my colleague at the university, Nina. She said that for a couple of weeks she had been working as an interpreter for a group of three young American directors who were invited to Poland by the ministry of culture to direct a play in one of Wrocław's professional theaters. She confessed that she didn't want to continue working with these people and that one of them asked if she could somehow get in touch with me. It turned out it was Travis whom I met a year earlier.

I went to see the Americans. Apart from Travis the trio consisted of Lloyd and Michael (lovingly called Spike). They were a bit brash, and very confident in their mission to dazzle the world (or at least Wrocław) with their creativity. However, their enthusiasm was very quickly tempered by various developments which proved to them that artistic work in a totalitarian country was not for the faint of heart.

To begin with, the proper authorities (i.e. censors) quickly communicated to them that their choice of material, a play by Sam Shepard, was not acceptable, because it was „too American". So they hastily settled on ancient Greek drama, „Prometheus Bound" by Aeschylus. This was accepted by the authorities, even though the play is in essence an account of a successful revolt of a persecuted individual (Prometheus) against a ruthless authoritarian (Zeus). I thought the acceptance of this text was more or less comparable to my legally obtaining a copy of „1984". In my case the rulers thought no one would read an English copy of Orwell's classic, and in the Americans' case they probably surmised that some ancient Greek text had to be „ideologically safe".

Secondly, Michael had some weird Polish visa problems

which down the line proved to be a major hassle and caused frequent contacts between him and the despondent crew working out of the ex-Gestapo red-brick building. More importantly, although all three Americans were in Poland on the invitation from the culture ministry, their work on an artistic project in a major Polish city caused heart palpitations in the ranks of spooks which was to become obvious very soon.

Travis, who was to be the director of the play, told me, to my surprise, that he tried repeatedly to get in touch with me, but was told by the theater administration that I was „not available". That was pretty strange and smacked of secret police interference, although it was impossible to find out what exactly happened. At that time I was engrossed in planning my final exit from Poland, and worked sporadically as a free-lance journalist. I also had very light teaching duties at my university, so I was obviously available to work with the Americans. I agreed to do so after Travis explained to me that he was not satisfied with Nina's performance as their interpreter.

The Americans also wanted me to translate into Polish a modern English-language reinterpretation of Aeschylus' original text. This was a very interesting project, because both the translation and the general direction of Americans' artistic work portrayed Prometheus as someone who was slowly gaining power over Zeus by mastering language. While I was no Prometheus, I clearly saw parallels between the play and my own life in communist Poland, and I also thought that the censors should have paid much more attention to the entire project. Luckily, they didn't.

The work involved was not easy. Every day, early in the morning, there were rehearsals during which I translated every single word spoken by either the American crew or the actors. The latter were a group of individuals difficult to handle, even without translating anything. Each of the actors had his or her peculiar traits and ambitions, so it was just a question of time before some major conflicts arose. There was also a growing number of disagreements and downright altercations between the directors and the actors. All of this in itself was difficult for me to navigate. But there were additional issues which very quickly resulted in almost total chaos.

For reasons difficult to understand, Ziggy and his bunch of goons came to the conclusion that the very presence of the three young Americans on a public stage was somehow a major threat. They started asking me for almost daily reports on what was happening during the rehearsals, which was silly since absolutely nothing was happening outside of routine banter between the actors and the „three American musketeers", as one of the SB agents kept calling them derisively. As a result, my day usually consisted of an interrogation at 7 am, followed by interpreting duties for the remainder of the morning. Travis, Michael and Lloyd started noticing that I was sometimes late for rehearsals and betrayed obvious signs of fatigue.

On top of that, the theater bosses, while initially very friendly, started doing almost anything in their power to thwart the production of the play. It was obvious that some of them were snitches for SB, but in the totalitarian soup of Poland it was difficult to separate meat from scum. The Americans became acutely aware of the fact that there were forces working towards their failure, and that a lot of people hanging around them might be informants.

One day I was walking towards the theater with the deputy director of that institution. We were just a few steps behind the three Americans, and he suddenly said to me with a smirk on his face: "Look at these three intellectuals". He was thus being offensive about people he knew absolutely nothing about, and the only explanation of his behavior was fear of possible competition, even though Travis and his friends were not in the running for any permanent positions at the theater. I won't mention the name of this theater official to spare him embarrassment, but on that day he behaved like a stinking, jealous coward. And so did his boss, who - after the Americans had left - invited me to a weird meeting in a hotel lobby (SB school of thought?) and asked me if I intended to sue the theater for copyright violations. Although there was reasonable ground to do that, I had no such plans. He asked me to write a letter to that effect, which I did, but in its last paragraph I expressed the view that the theater had treated its American guests atrociously, and should issue a formal apology to them. Of course no apology was ever given.

Both of these people went on to have successful careers - one of them in Poland, and the other one in the US. I never wished them any ill, but nothing will ever change the fact that back in 1979 they acted as dutiful subjects of a pitiful regime.

After two weeks of incessant turmoil I went with the Americans to a local dive called The Artists' Club, where very strange individuals got regularly drunk, and over a bunch of beers told them everything. I disclosed that I was being interrogated almost daily, that some people in the theater were almost certainly communist spies, and that my last remaining purpose in life was to get out of Poland for good. To the Americans all of that was a shocking revelation. In a sense, that night they lost their virginity, although not in any sexual way. They finally understood the parameters of their work in Poland.

Speaking of losing virginity, ensuing discussions between me and the US guests involved elaborate planning of getting me out of Poland. One of Travis's proposals was to get me married to an American woman. He had a candidate for such a daring mission, and he assured everyone that she would be ready not only to do this, but also to consummate the marital union, just in case anybody would want to check on that. There were also more exotic plans, like the one that would involve my traveling to the mountainous region of Bulgaria from where I would be sneaked across the border to Greece.

Needless to say, none of this ever happened. But in the course of those discussions I became friends with all three Americans, although my bond with Michael was the closest and most enduring - it persists to this very day. Half way through this tumultuous process Lloyd had had enough and decided to leave. Travis and Michael continued with their work, but the tensions kept rising, and at some point Travis was on the verge of a nervous breakdown. I engineered a weekend trip to the mountains south of Wrocław, and it seemed to help a lot.

At times the levels of stress and desperation of all three of us were such that we sought solace and relief in the aforementioned Artists' Club whose official name was Klub Związków Twórczych (Creative Unions Club). It was a very peculiar establishment hosting primarily actors, writers, and artists of all sorts, but also crawling with various suspicious types, including - I was sure - SB informants. Whenever we went there, we immediately ordered twelve beers, even though there were just three of us, because we knew the brew would run out pretty quickly. The club was always very noisy and at times shockingly weird. One time a drunken patron took off his pants and underwear, and climbed on the table to perform a dance of sorts, over dinner plates with food on them. Almost nobody reacted to this in any way. The constant chaos in that facility actually helped Travis, Michael, and I in relaxing after long days of rehearsals, and various conflicts associated with them.

Additionally, both Americans were introduced not only to my parents and siblings, but also to a bunch of my friends. Every now and then there were wild parties at my sister's place and it was very important, because these events started functioning as peculiar "release valves" for all the everyday tension and drama. During these parties we talked, drank a lot, danced, and often behaved like total fools, but that was probably just as well.

Unfortunately my situation was becoming worse by the minute. The secret police interrogators started threatening me with unspecified consequences if I didn't give them more information, whatever it was supposed to be. The rehearsal sessions were being discreetly „observed" by creepy individuals, and I and the two Americans were being followed by SB agents.

One day Michael was asked to report to the police headquarters to discuss his visa situation. He took me with him, hoping that I could be his translator. When we got there, the door to one of the offices opened, and a big, rude guy walked up to us. He looked at me and asked: "Who the hell are you?". When he heard about possibly interpreting Michael's interview, he told me to "back off and go home". My American friend spent about an hour talking to someone, most likely an SB agent, whose knowledge of English was farcically non-existent. It was therefore difficult to establish what actually happened, although the visa issue wasn't solved in any way.

This interview, together with many other incidents, was simply a campaign of intimidation. Sadly, the police guys were not the only culprits. The theater administration, including its director, inexplicably and abruptly fell out of love with their American guests. It was almost as if some higher authority told them to do whatever they could to thwart the entire project. And thwart they did.

Eventually „Prometheus Bound" had its Wrocław premiere in a hastily arranged space outside of the actual theater. It was a flop, which was probably the intended outcome. The production failed - not really artistically, but organizationally - and after a few shows it was closed down. The whole thing was a total mess, engineered by a bunch of scared autocrats and their even more scared underlings.

It should be noted that when it became obvious that the play would not be staged in the main theater building, Travis and Michael started looking for alternate venues and - unfortunately - someone mentioned to them the abandoned, half-finished rotunda, designated originally to house the "Panorama Racławicka" painting. I immediately told the Americans that the chances of getting this space for a theater production were basically none, but they insisted, attracted by the fact that the round building was presumably empty inside and could be provisionally turned into an interesting amphitheater.

On their request, I managed to schedule a meeting with the deputy head of the regional government, Danuta Wielebińska. Although - as far as I knew - she wasn't a typical communist party hack, it was obvious that she wouldn't be able to make any decision about the Americans' request even if she wanted to. The building was after all a taboo subject, and someone in Warsaw would have to OK using it for anything.

Our meeting with Ms. Wielebińska lasted about 60 seconds. When we walked into her office, Travis explained what he wanted to do and why. It produced an immediate response: "Absolutely not!". There was no further discussion and we were quickly ushered out of there. The rotunda remained censored.

After the premiere Travis, Michael and I decided to go on a train trip to Cracow and Gdańsk. This was supposed to be a goodbye tour for the Americans who were due to leave Poland a few days later. As the train was leaving Wrocław's main railroad station, Travis moonshined communism by sticking his naked ass out of the open window, which neatly summarized his state of mind. The trip was both exhilarating and tiring. Very early on I noticed that we were being followed by an SB agent whose face I immediately recognized. At that point we no longer cared - Travis and Michael were just about to go home, and I was staying behind in my own, miserable reality.

But the stupidity of the East Bloc wasn't done with the Americans yet. Travis and Michael planned to go to West Berlin, stay there for a couple of weeks, and then fly back to the US. My brother-in-law, Wojtek, volunteered to drive them to East Berlin in his plastic excuse for a car called Trabant (Trabi). When the three of them reached the border crossing between Poland and East Germany, they had no trouble clearing the Polish passport control. However, on the East German side of the Odra River the German guards stopped them and informed them that it was *verboten* for Americans to travel across GDR in cars shared with citizens of Warsaw Pact countries. So Wojtek turned around, drove into Poland again, to the merriment of the Polish officials, and then traveled with his "forbidden" passengers to a nearby railroad station where Travis and Michael boarded a train bound for Berlin.

Prior to these events I had some pretty emotional goodbye

hugs with my American friends. All three of us were more or less certain we will never see one another again, at least not in any foreseeable future. None of us could have known then that Poland was just about to dramatically change European geopolitics.

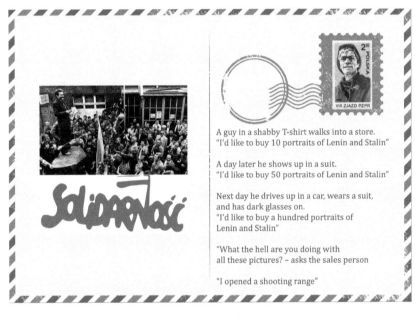

A guy in a shabby T-shirt walks into a store.
"I'd like to buy 10 portraits of Lenin and Stalin"

A day later he shows up in a suit.
"I'd like to buy 50 portraits of Lenin and Stalin"

Next day he drives up in a car, wears a suit,
and has dark glasses on.
"I'd like to buy a hundred portraits of
Lenin and Stalin"

"What the hell are you doing with
all these pictures? – asks the sales person

"I opened a shooting range"

Postcard no. 15 - Double revolution

After the Americans' departure my life was fast becoming tricky and untenable. Ziggy betrayed signs of growing paranoia about some imagined threats from the West. He was more demanding and aggressive, to the point of sometimes threatening me with arrest, although it seemed it was more bravado than real intent. One time he actually waved an arrest warrant in my face, but it only had my name on it, and the rest of the document was empty. At that point I asked him on what charges he would arrest me, and he responded that it didn't matter. He was right. They could invent crimes and produce "evidence", and I could end up in some dark cell with no recourse of any sort.

He also made it clear that any plans of studying in the US had to be shelved indefinitely as long as my cooperation with SB was not sufficient. It was impossible to figure out what sufficiency in this case meant. It was clear, however, that something changed for the worse as a result of my work with the American directors. As I learned many years later, Ziggy was actually pressured by his superiors to produce results, whatever they were supposed to be. It is therefore quite possible that he was a bit desperate, and wanted to move things along at any cost.

Meanwhile in early 1980 my relationship with Lucy grew to the point that we decided to get married in April of the same year. Exactly how that happened is difficult to elaborate on. The fact was that we started spending more time together, going out, talking, etc. I never proposed to Lucy, most likely out of fear of rejection. But one day, when we were both sipping a drink at a bar in Warsaw, she suddenly said very romantically: "So are you going to marry me or what?". How could anybody refuse such a direct offer?

The marriage was a major change, and a move that signified a temporary abandonment of plans to go to University of Illinois and to emigrate. My future bride had no idea about pressures from SB, nor did she know anything about my determination to some day leave Poland for good. The only person who knew some bits and pieces of all of that was my brother Tomek. While keeping Lucy in the dark was not very honest, it had its purpose. It was impossible to predict how the situation with Ziggy would develop, so it was safer to keep Lucy out of the loop just in case she got to be interrogated.

While travel to the US was out of the question, Lucy and I were allowed to make a short pre-wedding trip to London which was mostly devoted to shopping for things like bridal dress fabric, various accessories, etc. All of this was possible only because after my stint as a Russian teacher I stashed away some savings in a British bank and left the money there. Lucy was introduced to Sue and Louis for the first time, and also to Peter and Jean. It was a bit awkward, because she didn't speak a word of English, but it didn't seem to matter that much. At no time during this trip was the question of emigration mentioned or even alluded to. I am sure Ziggy knew I would never consider suddenly staying in the West while traveling with Lucy.

There were some important events before the wedding. Ewa, Lucyna, and Tomek graduated from their chemistry department in March of that year. Additionally Tomek announced his engagement to Ewa. Their wedding was scheduled just a few weeks after Lucy's and mine. All of us were thus on the threshold of adult, supposedly self-sufficient life.

The actual wedding ceremonies in both cases were great, despite the fact that almost everything was in short supply and procuring stuff was a difficult task. As for self-sufficiency, it was hard to achieve for a variety of reasons. Communist Poland had always struggled with acute housing shortages, so finding a place to live tended to be a major struggle. Most people rented small apartments at very steep prices, which is what Lucy and I did after we got married. The economic situation of Poland in 1980 was horrible and getting steadily worse, with rationing reaching new heights of absurdity. The shortages of virtually everything were rampant, the long lines in front of stores were still there, and prospects for any improvement remained very dim.

In the midst of all this my wife and I hosted unexpected visitors - Peter and Jean decided to come to Poland in late summer and we traveled with them to Cracow for a short tour of the city. All of this apparently rang some alarm bells in Ziggy's office, because he immediately demanded a meeting with me during which he voiced various concerns and asked for a spare key to the rented apartment in which the British guests were staying in Wrocław. He said that the apartment would be searched in Peter's and Jean's absence.

I gave him the key, and shortly afterwards warned Peter about the impending intrusion of the secret police. My Scottish friend reacted calmly and predictably: "I will leave all the dirty laundry on top of our things, plus a spent prophylactic to prove I am having sex with my fictitious wife" - he said. The search was done, and of course produced no results. Peter later said the searchers were so sloppy that he would have known they were there even if he hadn't been warned about it. Maybe they stole his condoms.

The guests left and a few weeks later a series of revolutionary events took place. In August shipyard workers in Gdańsk, angered by the announcement of major food price increases and dismissal of antigovernment activist Anna Walentynowicz, went on strike. This action spread like wildfire across Poland, so that by the last week of August Poland was totally paralyzed. The workers, under the leadership of Lech Wałęsa, published 21 demands, one of them being the establishment of a totally independent trade union called "Solidarność".

The government had no choice, but to agree. For the first time since the end of World War II a nation under the Soviet control won substantial concessions, and suddenly Poles had a mass organization free of the rulers' control. The country was full of enthusiasm and optimism, even though various people on both sides of the Iron Curtain warned that Moscow would not allow such a situation to continue.

In the first heady weeks after this revolt over 9 million people became "Solidarity" members. I didn't sign up. I was as enthusiastic about the developments in my country as everyone else, but in my entire life I never belonged to any organization, and I wasn't going to change that. I always thought that joining any mass political movement required some uncomfortable compromises, and in the case of "Solidarity" it was especially obvious. The ranks of the new trade union were full of people of all kinds of political affiliations and convictions, some of them pretty radical and controversial, like nationalists and neofascists, but also some anarchists and communists. Under normal circumstances I would never even consider meeting them, not to mention working with them.

Back in my high school years I was a member of an organization for about 15 minutes. I had a Russian teacher named Zoja who was a borderline psychopath. On some days she would behave quite normally, but every now and then she was vicious, mad, and vindictive. Once she walked into the classroom carrying a small box full of red ties. She distributed them among the students, asked them to put these things on, and then declared that as of then they were all members of Związek Młodzieży Socjalistycznej (Union of Socialist Youth), which was a breeding stable for young communists. Once I went home, I threw the tie away and thus my fleeting membership ended.

Of course in 1980 the situation was very different, because no Zoja told me to join "Solidarity", and the movement towards freedom was very real and spontaneous. Yet I decided to hold off until further developments. In the meantime the anticommunist revolt produced an immediate and welcome result - Ziggy stopped bothering me for a while, presumably busy with fighting internal "enemies of the state" as opposed to British and American spies.

For over a year, until the end of 1981, Poles lived in a

country which was dramatically different from what they got used to for decades. Censorship practically ceased to exist, independent newspapers were being published, and no one was afraid to say anything in public. There was a general feeling that may be, just may be, this time around the shape of postwar Europe would change for good.

These developments had a profound effect on me. I started thinking that perhaps emigration was no longer necessary and that I could continue living in my native land, freed from its Soviet yoke. I probably shared this view with millions of my hopeful compatriots. But as the months passed, there were all kinds of rumors about possible Soviet military intervention, the scenarios of which were written in 1956 Hungary and 1968 Czechoslovakia.

In February of 1981 there was another major development in our lives. Lucy and I welcomed to the world our son, Jakub. He didn't know it, but he was born in a country which was unexpectedly free, although nobody knew for how long. The hope was that all three of us would lead a relatively normal family life.

All this sudden optimism about the developments in Poland resulted in Lucyna and I inviting Sue and Louis to come and visit us in December of 1981. It was supposed to be a joyous, Christmas reunion back in the country in which I first met Sue. In preparation for this visit I stocked up on alcoholic beverages and various foods usually difficult to buy. Things in the country were still extremely challenging, but at least there was some hope of something better in the near future.

In my capacity of a journalist I met all kinds of people, across the Polish political spectrum, which in 1981 became tumultuous and unpredictable. One of these people was Kornel Morawiecki, the father of today's prime minister of Poland[1], Mateusz Morawiecki, and the leader of "Solidarność Walcząca" (Fighting Solidarity), which was a pretty radical splinter group. I thought Morawiecki was a bit crazy, because

[1] As of August 2023

117

in the midst of the shaky upheaval Poland was going through he and his allies advocated the immediate end of communism in Poland and other countries dominated by the Soviet Union, the break up of the Soviet Union, the separation of the USSR republics into new nation states, and the reunification of Germany within its Potsdam-imposed borders.

Even internally, within the Solidarity movement, some people thought he was nuts. Eventually all of these things did in fact come to pass, but in late 1981 Morawiecki's ideas seemed radical and totally unrealistic. On the other hand, Kornel - unlike some other activists - was never in favor of the use of violence to achieve his aims. For example, he thought, probably correctly, that mass hangings of communists on lampposts would solve absolutely nothing, perhaps because we didn't have enough lampposts in Poland.

One way or the other, during a couple of meetings I had with him he seemed to be absolutely convinced that communism in Europe was just about to collapse. It was an optimistic point of view, and I hoped he was right, but there were all kinds of signs that prophesied a different outcome.

A customer in an Warsaw auto parts store asks if they have tires for his car.

"We don't have any, but they have some in Wrocław. Here is a free ticket to Poznań"

"Why to Poznań?"

"Because that's where the queue ends"

Postcard no. 16 - A visitor from Washington

In October of 1981 I got a call from a friend in Warsaw who told me he wanted to employ me as a guide and interpreter for an American reporter who was just about to visit Poland for a few days. When he disclosed who this reporter was, I was shocked. It was Bob Woodward of "The Washington Post", the person who together with Carl Bernstein caused president Nixon to resign because of the Watergate scandal. Woodward was supposed to visit just two cities - Warsaw and Wrocław - and I got the job of accompanying him and translating his various meetings and press conferences.

Woodward struck me as a polite but aggresively inquisitive person who expressed keen interest in the situation in Poland. In Wrocław he had two major appearances - a press conference and a town hall style meeting with a large audience. The larger gathering produced many interesting questions from the audience - some of them were about Watergate, but some others concerned Woodward's views on the pro democracy awakening in Eastern Europe. The press conference was a much smaller event with Polish journalists as primary participants.

During this latter question-and-answer session, towards the end of the meeting, someone stood up and addressed everybody: "Don't you understand? We are working on borrowed time. It's all going to be over soon". This caused a bit of consternation, and Woodward asked me afterwards what that person meant. I explained to the American celebrity that there had been persistent rumors about some kind of drastic action on the part of the government against the "Solidarity" movement. Nobody knew anything concrete, and gossip ranged from a Soviet military intervention to the establishment of some sort of strict dictatorship.

In 2011, long after my name could be again freely mentioned, the press conference was related by Katarzyna Kaczorowska, a journalist working for "Gazeta Robotnicza". She wrote the following:

The Journalist Club was bursting at the seams. "Gazeta Robotnicza", the largest daily newspaper in the region, published a report on the press conference and an interview with Woodward, which was conducted by Andrzej Heyduk.

Woodward: "Talking to the journalists here, I embarrassed some of them, and talking to the workers confused me. I embarrassed the journalists with simple questions that they could not or would not answer."

Heyduk: "For example?"

Woodward: "For example, why can't you be impartial in everything you write, why can't you report facts without interpretation, why can't you hire half the journalists of a newsroom to work on one topic, for example the problem of food distribution or whatever? Why don't people believe you? I also asked you personally why your local television recorded an interview with me and it was not shown. You did not answer."

Heyduk: "Because I don't know why. Do you think that Poles can afford impartiality right now?"

Woodward: "You can always be impartial."

At this meeting Woodward said that the most important thing was the truth. Daniel Passent[2] asked him "but what truth?", telling the guest from across the ocean that there are two truths in Poland: government and "Solidarity".

It was true that the Wrocław TV station (totally controlled by the state) recorded an interview with Woodward during which I served as an interpreter. I have no idea why it was never broadcast, but it is almost certain that some "important people" intervened for whatever reasons. I never saw this interview, and I don't know if a copy of it still exists. However,

---

[2] A leading Polish journalist at that time.

I do remember that the American reporter basically said what he was more or less always saying - truth and objectivity matter, and they should be strived for regardless of costs. These were dangerous views even in the context of Poland in the midst of a pro-democracy revolution.

He was of course right in questioning the Polish journalists about their adherence, or lack thereof, to standard, western principles of news reporting. Unfortunately, he was also missing an important point, expressed by the mysterious commentator during the press conference. We all more or less knew that something pretty terrible was just about to happen which would make all the talk about press freedom moot.

It was late October and the situation in the country became extremely unstable. There was a series of strikes all over Poland, and some "Solidarity" leaders started expressing pretty radical views about the possibility of removing the communists from power by force (or by lampposts). The stores were virtually empty, with even rationed items in short supply. There was a general feeling that very soon something had to give, because things just couldn't continue like this any longer.

I told Woodward all about it. I then traveled with him to Warsaw where we were met by the "Washington Post" correspondent and a few other western journalists. There were all kinds of discussions among them and Woodward had a couple of additional public appearances. All of that was fascinating, but I came to the conclusion that the famous American guest didn't quite understand the enormity of what was happening in Poland.

One afternoon while walking around central Warsaw Woodward opined that the streets of the Polish capital were clean and well maintained. This astute observation was true, but totally irrelevant and unimportant. In late 1981 Poles couldn't care less about the cleanliness of their streets. They were in the middle of a dangerous, titanic power struggle with their communist overlords. It was an unprecedented situation which could cause serious, worldwide repercussions.

Additionally, Woodward somehow latched on to the idea that food distribution was a key factor of the situation in Poland. It wasn't, at least not at that time. To this very day I have no idea what he was talking about. Obviously, commercial food distribution in Poland was then totally controlled by the government, and no opposition forces were in any position to do anything about it. If someone were able to suddenly toss pork cutlets at the deprived populace, I am sure he or she would have scored a lot of political points. But it was all pie in the sky, and I was surprised that Woodward wasn't aware of that. We, the Poles, were trying to win and protect "life, liberty and the pursuit happiness", and not clean streets and efficient distribution of bacon and eggs.

On a purely personal level, I enjoyed the days spent with the universally known and admired journalist, and thanks to his visit I was introduced to a few foreign correspondents working in Warsaw. I also had some private conversations with Woodward in between various public appearances. It was fun to observe Bob in his element, asking questions in his very peculiar way which encouraged people to spill their guts almost inadvertently. I learned that he was an extremely meticulous and professionally cunning man. He talked to people very kindly and carefully, extracting information from them not through insistent questioning, but through rather loose, friendly conversation, during which his interlocutors shared their secrets with him.

As far as caution was concerned, Woodward absolutely never relied on the words of a single person. During many of our conversations he was always looking for separate confirmation of what I was telling him, and his talks with various important people in Poland at that time were consistently treated by him as "provisional data" that required a thorough check.

All in all, it was a great experience. But of course I understood that Woodward would pack his bags and return to the US, while I would remain in my country which was teetering precariously on the edge of some kind of precipice. I also understood that there was a huge divide between me and him - we had dramatically different biographies, careers, experiences, material circumstances, etc. And the biggest difference was that Bob never lived for a minute in a totalitarian state, whereas my life was totally stuck in it. That was pretty important. By that time I was already convinced that it was almost impossible for a citizen of a free society to fully understand what life in a totalitarian country was like without actually being there.

At the end of his stay in the city Woodward gave me a 100-dollar bill for my "services", saying that it wasn't a big deal, because he was rich. I accepted it, because in 1981 a hundred bucks in Poland was a lot of money on the black market (and in Pewex), and - yes - I knew that he was wealthy. However, it was a bit sad to see that he somehow viewed my helping him in monetary terms.

Once Woodward left, Lucy and I resumed preparations for the upcoming visit of Sue and Louis. Our guests successfully obtained Polish visas and bought airline tickets. Everything was more or less ready for their arrival.

Ziggy surfaced again, although this time he only called to ask if there was anything unusual about the American's visit. I answered, truthfully, that the visit was just a classic, quick fact-finding mission, and that I didn't observe anything out of the ordinary. The fact that this time Ziggy didn't want a face-to-face interview seemed odd. Also on the phone he sounded somewhat distracted and almost perfunctory which never happened before. I did not hear from him for months after that. Primarily because Ziggy would lose the capability of contacting anybody by phone. And so would I, as well as everybody else.

Jaruzelski is drowning in a river.
At the last moment he is saved by a teenage boy.
The grateful general asks him what
he would like as a thank you gift.
He answers that he wants a state funeral
with all the honors.

"Why are you thinking about
your funeral?" - asks Jaruzelski.

"Because when my dad discovers what I did,
he is going to fucking kill me".

Postcard no. 17 - Jaruzelski's war

1^{3th} of December 1981 was a cold and snowy Sunday day in Poland. It was also my birthday. I got up in the morning and switched the TV on. There was nothing on the screen except for electronic noise. I didn't think much of it, because things like that had happened before as a result of some technical glitches. At 7 am something did appear on TV.

General Wojciech Jaruzelski, then leader of the communist party and *de facto* head of state, delivered a 20 minute speech sitting in uniform against the background of weirdly crooked Polish flag. He announced to the nation that a "martial law" had been imposed overnight in the interest of "national security and stability". While initially it was difficult to understand what that actually meant, it turned out very quickly that Jaruzelski and his cronies started a war against their own nation.

Within hours almost 4 thousand people were arrested, and thousands more "interned". In all major cities soldiers, tanks, and personnel carriers appeared on the streets. "Solidarity" and most other independent organizations were shut down, all border crossings were closed, and telephone service was suspended indefinitely. The newly formed junta also introduced a curfew from 7 pm to 6 am, ordered all schools and colleges to stop classes, and prohibited the sale of any alcoholic beverages.

Jaruzelski's speech was broadcast a number of times, and when he was finally done, instead of normal programming the shocked viewers were served a steady stream of patriotic music, and messages from TV announcers dressed in military uniforms with no rank insignia. There was no way to contact anybody, and no way of doing practically anything else. When

Lucy got up, I told her the country was on war footing. "War with whom?" - she asked in justified disbelief.

A bit later we went for a walk with our little son who unbeknownst to him just stopped living in an increasingly free country and became a slave of a bleak military dictatorship. We saw only a few people in the streets, and one military patrol on foot. The three soldiers all wore battle ready gear, but they looked cold and dejected.

Since all the borders were shut down, it was obvious that Sue and Louis would not be coming for a visit. We couldn't get in touch with them, but correctly assumed that their Polish visas had been canceled. After a couple of days I went to the English Department at the university to see what was happening. Nothing was. The entrance door was guarded by a very young soldier with a machine gun at the ready. It was possible to walk in, but there were no students and no professors. Someone asked the soldier what he was doing there. He didn't say a word and looked confused. The country was frozen - both figuratively and physically. Everybody was stuck in bleak, frigid winter with just two weeks to go till Christmas.

There were some strikes and protests across the country, but they were quickly squashed with brute force by riot police. Some people died, many more were injured, but by the end of the year Jaruzelski and his thugs could claim that they regained control in the country. In reality Poland had been changed forever. After the initial shock of the martial law announcement, underground opposition groups started forming pretty quickly, very much like after the German invasion in 1939. "Solidarity" was officially disbanded, but it persisted in conspiratorial structures which became quite sophisticated. There were underground newspapers and magazines, independent books were being published, and even clandestine radio stations managed to broadcast every now and than thanks to equipment smuggled into Poland from the West.

All of that bore some resemblance to the way Home Army operated during WWII, although there were no open armed conflicts. The underground movement used some of the symbols and graphic signs originally designed by the fighters of AK back in the 40s. While the government reimposed heavy grip on the media, reintroducing strict censorship and totally controlling the flow of information, under the surface the country was bubbling with strong opposition and determination to fight against the new reality.

It was impossible to predict how long this fight would take and if it would ever succeed. And even if it did succeed, no one knew in what form that success would arrive. In December of 1981 hope was in short supply, and the ridiculously irritating hassle of everyday life tended to be overpowering. For the time being the Kremlin prevailed and forced a solution to "the Polish problem" without having to use the Red Army. To comrade Brezhnev that must have looked definitely like a success.

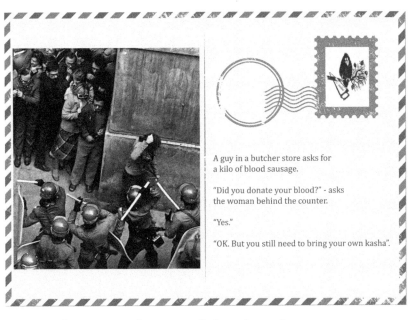

A guy in a butcher store asks for a kilo of blood sausage.

"Did you donate your blood?" - asks the woman behind the counter.

"Yes."

"OK. But you still need to bring your own kasha".

Postcard no. 18 - Theater of the absurd

For me the imposition of martial law was a major disaster. A few months earlier I had come to the conclusion that events in Poland had been heading towards peacefully changing the postwar division of Europe. I was hopeful that all the gains won since August of 1980 would be permanent and that my country would become a democracy, thus making my earlier emigration plans unnecessary. All of that was completely shattered.

I watched with growing alarm the return to the same bullshit propaganda I was hearing all my life. The authorities were doing whatever they could to erase the brief, 16-month pro democracy miracle from national consciousness. As early as in mid-1982 reading a Polish newspaper or watching TV news was more or less the same experience as 5 years earlier.

Faced with this, I started dreaming of leaving Poland once again, but my situation had become much worse. First, I now had a family, so whatever plans I might have or develop would have to take this into account. But, more importantly, as long as the junta maintained martial law, traveling to the West was simply impossible. The truth was that I was totally stuck and had no idea when a potential exodus from the country would become at least theoretically possible.

I was tired of waiting, and I was tired of my life being a part of a strange theater of the absurd. There were aspects of the restrictions introduced by the government which were not only stupid, but grotesque. Initially free movement of people between cities within Poland was severely curtailed. Lucy's parents were in Lubin. In order to go there, she had to apply to the local military commander for a special pass. Otherwise she couldn't board a train or a bus, and when traveling by car she would be stopped at the "border" between Wrocław and the rest of the country.

As for the phones, they remained silent until January 10th 1982. Then they started working again, but only for local connections. However, whenever someone made a call, he or she first heard a prerecorded phrase "rozmowa kontrolowana", i.e. "monitored conversation", which was a warning about the authorities eavesdropping. This was widely ridiculed for two reasons. First, Polish telephony was in such a shoddy state that listening to all the conversations was technically impossible. Second, telephone connections and correspondence were always "monitored" by the reds, although without any explicit warnings.

As always the Poles responded to their new predicament with humor, sometimes pretty morbid. One of the jokes ran like this. Ten minutes before 7 pm, i.e. just before curfew time, an old woman is trudging along the street. She is stopped by two soldiers who ask her for identification papers. She gives them her identity card, they examine it, and then one of them pulls out his gun and shoots her dead. "Why the hell did you do that?" - asks his colleague. "Oh, that's OK" - he answers - "I know where she lives. She would never have made it home by 7".

Jokes aside, the curfew had some strange consequences. Our son was prone to having asthma attacks which sometimes required medical intervention. Two weeks into martial law he suffered another such attack and had serious problems with breathing. It was 9 pm on a cold, winter day. Theoretically it was possible to call for an ambulance, even though the phones were dead. However, it was a moot point, because we didn't have a phone at home, very much like about 80% of the Polish population. So Lucy bundled little Jakub in warm clothes, and carried him in her arms on foot to the nearest hospital, traversing side streets and plowing her way through some bushes to avoid all the patrols. When she got to the hospital, the startled nurse on duty asked: "How the hell did you get here?".

After this incident many people throughout the years asked me why Lucy had gone with Jakub to the hospital and not me. The simplest answer I could give was (and still is) that once my wife decides to do something, she does it, come hell or high water. And hell certainly did come. However, there was also another explanation. The sight of a mother carrying her child, as opposed to the father, lowered a bit the chances of being shot on sight.

Although the situation was bleak, no members of our families or any of our friends got arrested. After a while, social contacts between people who knew and trusted one another resumed. Our place was for a while very popular, because we had a stash of vodka and beer, and prohibition was in force for weeks. There were some wild parties whose primary purpose was to forget about all that was happening in the country. On New Year's Eve my high school friend Maciek overdosed on booze, and wanted to deliver a speech to the nation from the balcony of our apartment, but was thankfully restrained.

We greeted the arrival of 1982 among our friends, but it was a very muted New Year celebration. None of us knew what would happen and where our country was going. It seemed obvious that for the time being all our hopes for a new Europe without the divisions agreed on back in 1945 had to be shelved indefinitely. And that was a devastating realization, because for a while it looked like freedom was just around the corner.

In these difficult times people stuck together and simply tried to survive all the restrictions and repression. The economic situation was getting progressively worse which was to be expected, especially in the face of sanctions against Poland, introduced by some states in the West, including America. Inflation was rampant, but in a perverse way it didn't really matter that much, because there was very little to buy. It was still possible to get some stuff at reluctantly tolerated open air markets where farmers sold things like meat, dairy, and fruit. One such market, round the corner from our apartment, sold eggs from time to time, and on one occasion I got two of them for my son after standing in line for over an hour. The socialist paradise crashed down to the level of hopeless absurdity.

Postcard no. 19 - Night heron

Black-crown night heron is a pretty bird with bright red eyes. The name of this creature in Polish is "ślepowron", which is strange, because it almost literally means "blind crow". It so happens, however, that the official name of Jaruzelski's junta was WRON (abbreviation of Wojskowa Rada Ocalenia Narodowego), i.e. Military Council of National Salvation, so it was no surprise to anyone that there was a myriad of jokes about blind crows, generals, military dictators, etc.

The imposition of martial law and subsequent clamp down on basic freedoms caused me to rethink my posture regarding being actively involved in anti-government activities. I decided that in order not to go bonkers in the new reality I had to do something, however insignificant, and that writing was probably the best option. So together with my friend Jacek, an architect and talented graphics artist, I joined a group working on an underground satirical magazine called "Ślepowron". There were some other people involved in the production and distribution of this periodical, but the gist of the undertaking was that I wrote and Jacek illustrated. Other writers also contributed to the magazine, but they were never identified. The irony of this was that the publication was sponsored by Kornel Morawiecki and his organization, so for a while I technically worked for the guy whom I suspected of being a radical whack job.

Being caught doing something like this meant an almost certain arrest and prison sentence, especially when Fighting Solidarity was involved. But Jacek and I didn't think about this too much, which was probably reckless on our part. The way our work was organized resembled to some extent the rules of conspiratorial activities during WWII, and that in itself gave me a pause. It was 1982 and we were involved in actions that were carried out very much like those 40 years earlier. The war was different, and the dictators were different, but the twisted irony of all this couldn't be more obvious. Each edition of "Ślepowron" was put together in a different apartment. We had no idea who normally lived in these places, and how they were procured. Once the magazine was finished, we handed it off for printing and distribution. We didn't know how many copies were being printed and where, and that's how it was supposed to be.

The publication of "Ślepowron" continued for almost a year, but then stopped, because there were suspicions that SB was on the trail of the entire publishing crew. All of this for me was very peculiar, because while I was writing for the magazine, I was also in renewed contact with Ziggy. Apparently my occasional interrogator had shaken off the jitters of his people chasing protesters in the streets and beating the hell out of them, and came back to his usual task of fighting against all the agents of Great Britain.

There were actually two days on which I talked to Ziggy in the morning and then went to work on "Ślepowron" in the afternoon. The surrealism of this situation was such that sometimes I had the urge of telling the SB dipshit sitting in front of me: "Hey, you know, as soon as we are done here, I am going to join my friends at a secret place and write some offensive satirical crap about you and your brainless goons". I never did say that, which was probably a good thing.

Jacek used his unquestionable talents in another way. He designed and meticulously made a fake, Polish 50-zloty banknote. It looked very authentic, except for the fact that the WWII era general, whose face adorned the currency, was replaced by a rather unflattering image of Jaruzelski, and the reverse side showed the Solidarity logo dripping with blood. Also the banknote was devalued to 50 groszy (Polish cents), although that was not very important, because even the real money was more or less worthless.

I had no idea who mass-produced the banknotes based on Jacek's design, and how they did it , but we all passed the fake money around, even though doing that sort of thing in any country is a crime. This obviously wasn't done for any material gain. It was a part of our own propaganda war. One rainy night I was traveling by taxi, and the driver offered his own take on the meteorological situation by saying "Look at how the rain is pissing on this commune". Encouraged by his thinly veiled political statement, at the end of the ride I gave him two 50-zloty banknotes - one real, and one fake. He looked at them, smiled, and gave the real one back to me. "Thank you" - he said.

After a while it became obvious that all the martial law stuff was weighing heavily on Ziggy's fragmentary mind, because every now and then he couldn't resist saying things that sounded like complaints or grievances. At one point he complained that people tended to treat all security services as a single entity, thus throwing him into the same basket as the so-called ZOMO (Motorized Units of Citizens' Militia), i.e. the hated riot police, consisting of brutal thugs and responsible for violent attacks against "enemies of the state". He was obviously suggesting that the gorillas of ZOMO had nothing to do with the "intelligentsia" of SB. On another occasion he alluded to the supposedly unjust way in which his organization was being portrayed in the opposition circles.

It seemed that Ziggy was beginning to understand that things were rapidly changing in Poland, despite the temporary suppression of "Solidarity", and that the day might come when his services would no longer be needed. Perhaps he even entertained the possibility that one day he might actually be prosecuted. He never was. But when communism fell in 1989 and SB was dissolved, he applied for a position in the new security service, thinking perhaps that the work would be the same, but under different bosses. He was told to fuck off.

On the last day of August 1982, the second anniversary of the birth of "Solidarity", there were huge and sometimes violent demonstrations in Wrocław. Around noon thousands of people showed up in the streets to demand that "Solidarity" be legalized again. The demonstrators also wanted freedom for all the political prisoners, and return to the agreement signed with the striking workers in August of 1980.

Protesters were met by ZOMO in full force. In various spots clashes erupted, and in some cases there were pitched battles between the police and the demonstrators. On the Grunwaldzki Bridge over the Odra River there were police vehicles burning. Most of city center was enveloped in clouds of tear gas, and police helicopters were circling above. The streets reverberated with the sounds of police and ambulance sirens. It was a total pandemonium.

For hours Wrocław resembled a war zone. The riots and open battles died down at sunset, but the streets were strewn with all kinds of debris for a few days. The opposition made its point. At around the same time the last issue of "Ślepowron" was published and distributed. It was obvious to everybody that, contrary to official propaganda, martial law did not solve anything and left Poland in a sharply divided, precarious state.

Postcard no. 20 - The Australian connection

Half way through 1982 telephones started working again for inter city connections, but no international calls were allowed. Although that wasn't quite true. Foreign correspondents working in Poland could call anybody in the world, but they had to first dial a special number given to them by the authorities, and the connection was then established for them. I had no idea about any of this until one day I was contacted by one of the western journalists in Warsaw whom I met during the Woodward visit.

Mike worked for the British weekly "The Economist" and called me just to say hello and ask whether I was OK. During our short conversation he mentioned the fact that he could call numbers outside of Poland and - if needed - he would allow me to get in touch with whomever I wanted, although I would have to get to Warsaw to do that. I did that and called Sue in London. She was very surprised. We talked only for a few minutes, during which time Sue bombarded me with questions, and at the end of all this asked me if I needed anything. The obvious answer under the circumstances would be "everything", but I just said that it would be great if she could send us some canned food for our son. I had no idea if that was even possible.

What I didn't know was that in places like Chicago, London, Paris, and Berlin thousands of people organized shipments of food parcels to Poland and offered their services to whoever wanted to send something. After a few weeks Lucy and I received a package from London, containing not only stuff for our son, but also cocoa, tea, coffee, chocolate, sugar, etc. It was a very welcome surprise, but also brought with it a somber realization that the socialist paradise had to be aided by the "rotten" West.

While in Warsaw, I was invited by Mike to dinner at a restaurant in the city center. There were about 5 other people, all of them westerners. Surprisingly, Walter was one of the participants of this gathering. While eating and drinking, they all talked about current events, general situation in Poland and abroad, prospects for the future, etc. Since I was the only Polish diner, they peppered me with questions, not only about my views on Jaruzelski's war, but also about my personal situation and plans. I didn't hold back, explaining that the imposition of martial law demolished my hopes for the future and that I wanted to emigrate as soon as possible. Everybody knew that for the time being that was impossible. Except for the Australian.

"If you really want to leave, you need to start working on it immediately. Sooner or later martial law will end, and by that time you should be ready" - he said.

"Ready for what?"

"Sorry, I said it wrongly. You should make **them** ready to let you go."

"I have no idea what you are talking about".

"That's OK. When are you leaving Warsaw?"

"Tomorrow afternoon".

"Let's get together somewhere tomorrow morning, and we'll talk more".

The following day we met in the foyer of Hotel Bristol. Sitting at a table in a pretty secluded spot, Walter explained what he meant the day before.

"Basically you need to convince the SB people that as soon as you go to America or Great Britain you will be recruited by one of their intelligence services. If you succeed in doing that, they will gladly send you out, hoping that they will get a valuable asset."

I listened to this with growing disbelief.

"Sorry, but I think this is nuts" - I said - "How can I possibly convince these people that someone in the West will recruit me? What possible value could they see in me?"

"It's simple. You speak excellent English and you know a lot of people like me. All you need is some valid pretext to go to the West."

"I have one. University of Illinois accepted me for their PhD program. I have the necessary papers and I actually want to do that."

"That's great. Right now these papers are worthless, because under martial law you can't go anywhere. But their day will come. Listen, I will help you. Together with a few other people".

"Help me how? And why?"

"As for why, it doesn't matter. As for how, don't worry. I am not talking about shooting your way through the border or stuffing you in a lorry going to West Berlin".

"So what exactly are you talking about?"

"Let's do this. I am going to come to Wrocław in a couple of weeks. Let the person you are talking to at SB know about my visit. And then select some public place where we will meet. Like a bar or a restaurant. Are you OK with that?"

"Yes."

I went back home in a state of some bewilderment. Walter's offer to help was baffling, because we barely knew each other. And the idea of convincing Ziggy and his pals about my imminent recruitment by foreign spy agencies seemed to be pretty far-fetched.

As promised, Walter called me after a while and told me he was coming for a visit. He was staying at Hotel Monopol, so we agreed to meet at the restaurant on the ground floor of the same building. As instructed, I informed Ziggy about the Australian visitor, and I could sense that the news puzzled him. He wanted to know why Walter was coming. I told him that I didn't know, and in large measure that was true.

At the restaurant Walter first told me that he was certain we were being watched, but assured me they couldn't hear us. Then he proceeded to explain his plan. He was going to organize a series of meetings between me and various westerners, primarily in Wrocław, so that with time SB would start thinking I was being pursued by foreign agents.

The meetings were supposed to be held in public spaces, always one-on-one. I would not inform Ziggy in advance about these encounters, but - if asked - I was free to tell him about what was discussed. With some embellishments. Walter suggested that I should feed Ziggy the narrative of successive foreigners asking me in a roundabout way whether I would be willing to provide information and come to the West to learn more about what kind of information was needed and how to get it. He offered to help me "putting together" such a narrative.

This led me to a rather obvious question.

"What will I be talking with these people about?" - I asked.

"O dupie Maryni" - answered the Australian in decent Polish.

I couldn't help laughing, because I didn't expect that Walter would know this expression. In Polish the phrase "rozmawiać o dupie Maryni" literally means "to talk about Mary's ass", but is meant to describe conversations about nothing or about meaningless trivialities. That is how my Australian acquaintance imagined the discussions during the meetings. He also said that people coming to meet with me would be reporters from English-speaking countries. With one exception.

"Eventually you will also meet with one guy who is an active agent of a foreign intelligence service. You will not know his name, and he is not going to talk to you about recruitment. You will just exchange the usual crap with him. What counts is the visual of your getting together with him."

"Dare I ask how you know this person?" - I asked.

"You can certainly dare, but I won't answer. Are you willing to do this?"

All of this was pretty weird, but I had nothing to lose by agreeing to Walter's plan. I thought the chances of success were pretty remote, but if for some reason the ruse worked, I might end up in Chicago. This was happening in the fall of 1982, and the first meeting was supposed to be held before Christmas of the same year.

Before we left Monopol restaurant, I asked one last

question.

"Tell me, Walter, what's in it for you? Why are you willing to do all this for someone like me? You practically don't know who I am."

Walter smiled briefly and somewhat furtively.

"I am not doing this for you. I need to know if a plan like this can actually work in a country like this. So, sorry, but in reality you are my guinea pig."

"Good to know. Thanks, I feel much better now."

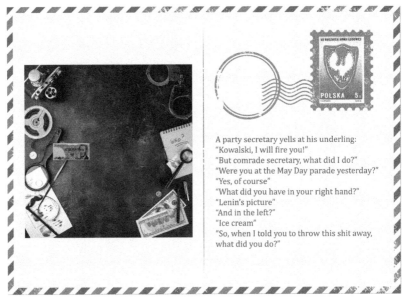

A party secretary yells at his underling:
"Kowalski, I will fire you!"
"But comrade secretary, what did I do?"
"Were you at the May Day parade yesterday?"
"Yes, of course"
"What did you have in your right hand?"
"Lenin's picture"
"And in the left?"
"Ice cream"
"So, when I told you to throw this shit away, what did you do?"

Postcard no. 21 - About Mary's ass

Towards the end of 1982 rumors started circulating about the possible suspension of martial law. This indeed happened on the 19th of December. A lot of previously imposed restrictions were lifted, so life became somewhat easier. Seven months later, on the 22nd of July, Jaruzelski decided to cancel his military rule altogether. The date chosen for this decision was no accident.

In communist Poland that particular day was a national holiday, because on the 22nd of July 1944 an organization called Polski Komitet Wyzwolenia Narodowego (PKWN), i.e. Polish Committee of National Liberation, was formed. It was essentially a provisional, communist council, created by Stalin to counter the government in exile functioning in London. PKWN, under a watchful eye of Soviet NKVD, took control of the areas liberated by the Red Army. The organization was full of Polish communists trained in Moscow who would eventually become the new rulers of PRL.

On the 39th anniversary of putting a bunch of Kremlin stooges in charge, their descendants canceled martial law. It was an odd birthday present which was largely meaningless, because the country just went back to where it started - to a sham proletarian paradise. However, for me there was one important consequence of those developments - foreign travel became possible, at least theoretically, so admission papers to University of Illinois once again became important.

As planned, in December of 1982 I had my first meeting with a foreign reporter. We got together in a bar where he introduced himself as Adam from "The Boston Globe". For about an hour we talked about the weather, sports, and Polish food - in other words, we talked about Mary's ass while having a few beers.

More meetings like this followed in relatively quick succession. Most of the people showing up were Americans, but there was also Ian from "The Daily Telegraph" in London, and George, apparently working for "The Toronto Star" in Canada. Of course I had no way of knowing whether I was talking to real journalists and whether they were giving me their real names. During some sessions I and my conversation partners would huddle closely together over a small table, and talk very quietly, almost whispering. This was done on purpose, per Walter's wishes.

It didn't take a long time for Ziggy to become interested. He started asking for information on what was being discussed in the meetings, and this time I didn't have any problem with providing it. Sticking to Walter's narrative, I kept dropping vague hints about the foreigners' interest in my family and my possible willingness to leave my wife and son behind for an extended period of time, should such a need arise. I also told Ziggy that one of the journalists suggested that I could work with "important people on a variety of issues".

No such matters were ever discussed or mentioned during the get-togethers, but that didn't matter. After about 5th meeting, in March of 1983, I told Ziggy that one of the reporters asked me when I thought it would be possible to travel to the West to meet "certain interested individuals". I lied like hell and never thought twice about it. It was a risky game, and I certainly didn't know all the players, nor did I have any idea about what their real intentions were. But these were desperate times, and I was ready to do almost anything to accomplish my ultimate goal.

Finally, in early April I met the "real agent". He was a tall American in his fifties who spoke with a southern accent. The meeting was not very different from all the previous ones, expect for the fact that the guy was very serious, didn't talk much, and left after about half an hour. Additionally, we didn't meet in any enclosed space, but in a park where we sat on one of the benches. It was a rather incongruous situation which reminded me of various encounters between fictional characters in mediocre spy movies.

If Walter assumed that the SB people knew who this

person was, he was probably right, because the following day Ziggy requested an urgent meeting with me and basically told me that I had been talking to an active CIA operative based in the US embassy in Warsaw. In response I played dumb, said I knew nothing about it, and added that the American didn't say anything important and didn't ask me any suspicious questions, except for one. He wanted to know where I would go in the US if I ever came for a visit. The answer was Chicago. Of course this was a blatant lie, because no such question was asked.

The meetings arranged by Walter ended, and Ziggy faded away for a while. The Australian also dropped out of sight. This unfortunately meant that SB didn't take the bait, and the plan didn't move forward even an inch. But then a miracle happened.

In mid-April Ziggy asked me to attend a meeting with him and his superior, a colonel in SB. Nothing like this ever happened before, and it was difficult to figure out what the purpose of such a meeting could be. On instructions from Ziggy, I went to Hotel Panorama, and knocked on the door of a "designated" room where, apart from Ziggy, I found another guy. The man was heavy set and bald, and he didn't bother to introduce himself. We all took seats around a small table, and Ziggy produced a bottle of "Jarzębiak", a flavored vodka which I detested.

We each had a shot of this crap, and then the colonel started talking. What he had to say was nothing short of amazing.

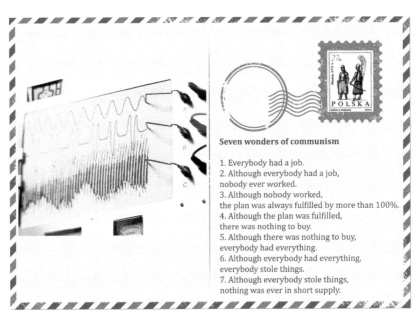

Seven wonders of communism

1. Everybody had a job.
2. Although everybody had a job, nobody ever worked.
3. Although nobody worked, the plan was always fulfilled by more than 100%.
4. Although the plan was fulfilled, there was nothing to buy.
5. Although there was nothing to buy, everybody had everything.
6. Although everybody had everything, everybody stole things.
7. Although everybody stole things, nothing was ever in short supply.

Postcard no. 22 - Hook, line, and sinker

Ziggy's boss started by saying that he was very appreciative of all the information I gave them, and expressed his hope that this cooperation would continue. Little did he know that most of the stuff I offered them was simply fake. Almost immediately after that he delivered a short speech during which he explained that SB was not interested, and never would be interested, in training me as an agent and employing me. However, he added that there were certain events and pieces of information which caused them to think that I was being actively pursued by foreign intelligence services and that sooner or later they might want to recruit me.

Then the following shocking conversation followed.

"We understand that you were accepted for doctoral studies in the US. Is that right?"

"Yes."

"How long does something like this take?"

"It's difficult to predict. Usually at least three years."

"And you have a wife and a young child?"

"Yes."

"All right. Would you be willing to go to the States to study?"

I could hardly believe my ears, and found it difficult to hide my excitement. Once I picked up scattered wits from my brain's floor, I responded very cautiously.

"Well, I don't know. I need to think about it. First of all, I cannot leave my family behind for such a long time. Secondly, and I will be blunt, I assume that you would like me to go to Chicago and work for you in some fashion."

"Yes, but only to some extent. We are more or less sure that you would be approached by someone working for the CIA or FBI or whatever. All we would ask you to do is to relay to us all the information about such contacts. And if they ask you to do something specific for them, we would like to know about it."

"And then do what they ask?"

"Maybe. It depends on what they would ask, but we would let you know."

"What if I am not approached by anybody?"

"Then you complete your studies and come back. No problem."

"Right. As I said, I am not sure I want to go. Can I have a few days to think about it?"

"Sure. If you do agree to go, there are some preparations we need to go through."

"What preparations?"

"Doesn't matter right now. We'll talk about it later".

At this point Ziggy poured everyone another shot which we quickly consumed. Then I got up and left them. When I got out of the hotel and started walking towards my university, I felt literally dizzy, but not because of "Jarzębiak". It seemed that Walter's plan had just worked, despite very long odds. However, this success wasn't complete yet. I never told my wife about my emigration plans and didn't intend to. So if I went to the US, I needed some assurance, however flimsy, that Lucy and Jakub would be able to join me.

There was a very important reason for that. A while back, before martial law was introduced, especially during my work with the three Americans, my life became miserable and hopelessly entangled with my role of a liaison between SB and a bunch of foreigners. On top of that, Jaruzelski's war brought even more grief and caused me to delve into underground activities, albeit for a relatively short time.

I therefore decided that if I ever made it to the US, I would almost immediately apply for political asylum. My intentions were risky in two ways. First, if asylum was denied, I would most likely be deported immediately back to Poland. Second, if it was granted, I would not be able to go back to Poland for a very long time, if ever. Assuming optimistically that the asylum application would be successful, I needed some way to get my family to the US in relatively short order.

After a few days Ziggy got in touch with me again and asked me whether I made any decisions. I responded that the biggest obstacle for me was leaving my family behind. Ziggy's reaction was surprising. He said that there was a law in Poland which specifically said that people who stay abroad to study or work for more than six months have the right to bring their immediate family over. I had no idea whether such law really existed (it did), and I also knew very well that any law could easily be ignored or violated by the government on any pretext. But the fact that Ziggy even mentioned this rule was certainly a positive sign.

For the next few weeks I dithered, hoping that perhaps Walter would show up again and advise me on what to do. But the Australian vanished into thin air. In fact I never saw him again, and to this day I don't know who he was and why he did what he did. So, left to my own resources, I eventually told Ziggy I was going to study in the US as long as my family would be able to join me. At the same time I reached out to the Philosophy Department at University of Illinois to verify that I could join the graduate program in the fall of 1983.

The next few months were downright weird. I started having conversations with Ziggy about what to do and not to do while in the United States. I was also told that if I needed urgent help with anything, I could call a "special number" in the Polish consulate in Chicago, so that someone could meet me and discuss the issue. I went along with this game, but I had absolutely no intention of calling any representative of the government from whose clutches I was trying to extricate myself.

In June Ziggy suddenly said that we needed to go together to the town of Leszno, about 60 miles north of Wrocław, where SB apparently had a "facility" of some sort. He explained that they needed to hook me up to an American made lie detector in order to train me on the art of passing the test even when lying. It seemed to be a very odd move on the part of SB, but at that stage the only thing I could do was to comply.

The facility turned out to be an ugly barrack hidden in the

163

woods. There was a technician who was waiting for us inside. He led me into a small room and hooked me up to the lie detector via a bunch of wires. He also put two belts around my chest. Before the actual test started, the technician said that the general idea behind trying to determine whether someone was lying or not was that the interrogator asked questions and when somebody lied, he or she got more stressed than when telling the truth. This difference would be revealed in the physiological indications, such as pulse, brain activity, blood pressure, breathing rate, etc.

Then he said this: "A simple way to cheat the polygraph is to deliberately distort your physiological readings when telling the truth, such as by biting your tongue, pinching yourself or imagining an embarrassing or painful incident in the past. That way the difference in physiological states of lying and truth telling gets blurred".

"Great" - I thought - "All I have to do is to think of sister Maria without her habit." The technician explained that he was going to ask fifty questions and that the answer was always either yes or no. He also encouraged me to deliberately lie every now and then. Without further ado, he started the session. The questions ranged from "Were you born in 1953?", through "Have you ever had a sexual encounter with a man?" to "Are you now or have you ever been an SB agent?".

All of this was a totally pointless and colossally stupid exercise, because I was absolutely certain I was never going to be subjected to a lie detector test in the US, but I couldn't just say I didn't want to do it. So I played along. Having answered all the questions, I was disconnected from the machine, and went back to Wrocław with Ziggy. I never heard about any results of the test, and therefore I never found out whether my deliberate lies were correctly detected. In particular, I never learned if the machine believed me when I answered 'yes' to the question about having sex with a guy.

After this bizarre trip I applied for and got my passport, which this time around wasn't a big surprise. There was also no problem with obtaining American student visa. In late June

I bought a Polish Airlines LOT ticket to Montreal for September 9th. I couldn't fly directly to Chicago, because earlier president Reagan had slapped a ban on LOT as a sanction for imposing martial law. But a changeover in Canada didn't matter. I was finally on my way out of Poland.

As far as Lucy was concerned, all she knew was that I was going to America to study, and that she would be able to join me together with our son after a few months. She was absolutely convinced that our stay in the US would be temporary. In fact nobody knew about my true intentions except for my brother, but even he was aware of just fragments, and not the whole story.

Everything was ready for the final exit. However, the summer of 1983 turned out to be pretty hot, although not in any meteorological sense.

An ambulance pulls up to hospital ER
with wounded ZOMO riot policemen.
As they are being taken out,
a woman starts crying.

"Why are you so emotional about them?" - asks
another bystander.

"How can I not cry when I see that
the ambulance has capacity to take 5 policemen,
but brought only two?"

Postcard no. 23 - Final turbulence

It wouldn't be an exaggeration to say that in the spring of 1983 Poland was in a very sad state. Almost three years of martial law seemed to have squashed opposition, but only on the surface. There had been absolutely no concrete improvements in the daily lives of ordinary people, and the economic situation was tragic. Under such dire circumstances the government propagandists were hard-pressed to say anything coherent. And yet they tried. The media regularly proclaimed that everything was totally peachy and that major progress was being made towards peace and prosperity. Most of Poles knew it was total baloney.

On the first of May 1983 there was the usual May Day parade. Throngs of people carrying banners with moronic slogans marched down one of the main streets of Wrocław, in front of a viewing stand populated by local dignitaries and two generals - one Polish and one Soviet. But this was not meant to be an ordinary celebration.

The opposition infiltrated the marching crowd, and once their people were in front of the viewing stand, they unfurled their flags, started singing the Polish national anthem, and chanted slogans which could be diplomatically called "hostile" to the rulers. The party dignitaries looked somewhat confused, but that wasn't their biggest problem. The ZOMO riot police was ordered to attack the opposition demonstrators. And they did just that, with their usual zeal, using lots of tear gas which didn't recognize any ideological distinctions and drifted recklessly towards the viewing stand. The communist honchos and the generals had to hastily retreat, with some of them crying profusely.

Fighting in the streets of Wrocław lasted for hours. Over

400 people were arrested and one person died when he was hit in the chest by a tear gas canister. It was one of the most unusual May Day parades in the history of PRL, and it showed that the projected facade of stability was a total myth. A few days after these events Ziggy, who kept quiet for a while, met me and showed me about 10 photographs of the May Day demonstrators. He wanted me to look at the pictures to see if I would recognize anybody.

This represented a departure from the usual behavior by Ziggy. He never showed me any photos before, and never asked me to identify people taking part in opposition activities. Somehow, at least for the time being, British and American spies became less important to him. I looked at the photos, which were a bit blurry. I did recognize a friend of mine, but with a straight face I told Ziggy I didn't know any of the demonstrators.

Six weeks later, on June 16th, Pope John Paul II came for his second visit to his native land. His presence in Poland was a risky proposition for the government, because for a few days the pontiff was supposed to travel around the country and during this time he had an open platform from which he could address the nation in any way he wanted, uncensored. Obviously he couldn't say things like "Go to the streets and chase these communist perverts out", but in a way he more or less said the same thing in a different way.

It was estimated that during his pilgrimage over 10 million Poles listened to what he wanted to say. While I didn't care about all the religious stuff, it was impossible to overlook the fact that he represented an important, independent voice, and that he used his open air masses to preach hope. He told the nation that they needed to persevere and hope for a better tomorrow, because the tyranny would eventually pass and be replaced by brighter times. He was predicting that communism would simply collapse, but unfortunately he couldn't give anybody any specific dates.

The pope came to Wrocław for one day, on June 21st, and his mass on the outskirts of the city was attended by well over 100 thousand people. During the papal visit I worked as a translator in the press office, and because of that role I found myself briefly in the presence of the pontiff, together with a bunch of other people. We were all in one of the large rooms of Wrocław archbishop's residence, standing in a neatly arranged row of interpreters and reporters. The pope walked in, waved to us from a distance of about 20 feet, and walked slowly past to an exit door. This very short encounter with the head of the Catholic church and the earthly deputy of God did not influence my feelings about religion in any way. However, I half expected that the following morning Ziggy would demand a meeting during which he would tell me that the pope was a secret agent for the Italian AISE (equivalent of SB), and that he was surreptitiously married to Jean, Peter's fictitious wife. But this time Ziggy kept silent.

Some predicted that the pope's presence would provoke renewed anti-government demonstrations and street riots, but nothing like that happened. Perhaps one of the reasons was that the underground "Solidarity" structures in Wrocław had been weakened by arrests of a few important leaders. But there was also another reason. People in Poland slowly resigned themselves to the prospect of communism continuing for a while. It was impossible to predict for how long, which resulted in a growing feeling of apathy and discouragement.

On the third anniversary of the creation of "Solidarity", just 9 days before my scheduled departure for the US, there were still street demonstrations and protests, but on a much lesser scale than in the previous year. It seemed that the appetite for open struggle with Jaruzelski and his goons had waned. This was very discouraging and enforced my conviction that emigration was the only option, regardless of possible difficulties and complications.

I was counting the days off and was ready to go. I saw Ziggy briefly at the end of August, but the main purpose of that quick get-together was for him to check off all the items on the list that he was supposed to cover as preparation for the trip to the United States. Once again he rattled off some basic instructions about what to do and what not to do when confronted with possible recruitment efforts by American special services. I didn't know it then, but that was the last time I would see Ziggy in my life. Not a day too soon.

What would we have if there was no PRL?

Everything!

Postcard no. 24 - Adieu

The time finally arrived. In the early morning on the 9th of September 1983 Lucy and I boarded a train to Warsaw. After a few hours we emerged from the railroad station in the center of the city, and took a taxi to the Okęcie airport. We said our goodbyes just before I boarded the plane. I didn't really know what to do, so I simply turned to Lucy and said "Hope to see you soon". The problem was that I didn't really know if that would turn out to be possible.

As the plane was taking off, I looked out of the window at the decrepit airport terminal and thought: "This is the last fucking time I'm leaving this place". It wasn't the last time. I couldn't have known that in just six short years communism in Eastern Europe would collapse, and all the reasons for my emigration would disappear. But that didn't matter. I was finally on my way to the New World. But I was also leaving behind my wife and son, my aging parents, close family members, and lots of friends. Basically, I was leaving everything. In my suitcase I had a change of clothes for 5 days, a few books, and some toiletries. In my pockets I had nothing - most importantly, I had no money other than a few dollars.

After a 9 hour flight, a changeover in Montreal, and another two hours in the air, I landed at O'Hare airport in Chicago. Three weeks later I started my studies at the University of Illinois where I met many wonderful people, including two who are my close friends to this very day. The next 6 months were trying, to say the least. The first thing to do was to send proper papers to Lucy in Poland, so that she could apply for an F-2 visa, given to spouses and children of full time students. But of course first she needed to apply for her passport, and that was the trickiest part.

While all of that was happening, I hired an immigration lawyer, trying to put together the asylum application. I needed to tread carefully - my plan was to actually file the application only after Lucy got her passport and visa. The lawyer was a young woman who listened to my story and then warned me that asylum cases were notoriously difficult for a simple reason - typically applicants didn't have any proof of danger or persecution, so it was their words against the beliefs and policies of the US government. She added that the success ratio of such applications was about 20%.

However, my case was a little bit different. I re-established contact with Travis and Michael, both of whom were shocked to hear from me again. In fact Michael was convinced that I was either dead or imprisoned. Anyway, they agreed to write supporting statements to be included with the asylum application. One person who didn't agree to write any statement was Bob Woodward. I wrote to him and asked him for a brief note stating that we met in Poland, and that he could confirm my identity. I also sent him my statement which I was going to file with the application for asylum. In response Bob called me and told me that he couldn't do that, because if it turned out that I was a communist spy, it would be detrimental to his professional career. Curiously, he added that I could just be an inadvertent spy, whatever that was supposed to mean. Woodward's answer was disappointing, but to some extent understandable.

By January of 1984 all the paperwork for asylum was ready. A month later I got the news that Lucy and Jakub got their passports and American visas. They were supposed to join me on the 9th of March 1984. Given all of this, I had a choice to make. Initially I intended to file the asylum application just before my wife's arrival, but then, after consulting with my lawyer, it seemed that doing that after Lucy and Jakub got to the US was a safer option. And that's what I did.

My wife and son landed at O'Hare as planned. I took them to the small apartment that I had rented earlier. After some celebratory drinks, I turned to Lucy and uttered words that would live in family infamy forever: "Honey, there is a slight change of plans". And with that phrase the chapter of our lives in PRL was shut down, and a new chapter began.

Lucy initially was too shocked, tired, and confused to hit me with something heavy over the head or voice loud verbal complaints. But this event weighed heavily on our marriage for quite some time to come. It was understandable - I engaged in an act of trickery and deceit which I thought was necessary. That, however, didn't absolve me from guilt.

In late March the asylum application was filed. One stage of this entire process was that all asylum applicants had to appear in front of an immigration officer for an interview. So one day I, accompanied by my lawyer, showed up at the Dirksen Federal Building in downtown Chicago. After a short wait we were seated at a desk and joined by a serious looking woman.

It was obvious almost from the very beginning that the INS official didn't read a word of the underlying documentation. She was asking a series of routine questions which were probably on some list of the questions to be asked. Eventually the following conversation occurred.

"So you graduated from college in your country, right?"

"Yes."

"Well, that means that you had to be a member of the communist party".

"Excuse me?"

"We know that only party members are admitted to colleges in Bulgaria".

"I am from Poland".

"Doesn't matter. It's all the same."

"Well, if I may, your information is not correct. Party membership has never been required as a condition of college admission. Either in Poland or Bulgaria".

"As I said, we know this to be a fact".

There was absolutely no point in continuing this discussion. The woman asked a few more questions, shuffled through the pages that she never read, and then said:

"OK, I will send this on to the Department of State, but

honestly I see no chance of this application being approved".

The interview obviously didn't go very well and I was dejected. There was nothing else we could do but wait. However, it was strangely reassuring to find out that stupid bureaucrats existed everywhere, regardless of the political system. In the meantime in May I decided to "clear the air" with Woodward by sending him a letter. I thought I had to send it, and writing it actually helped me understand that in my new country people may question my past and have doubts about it. The letter in part said this:

Dear Bob.

Sorry to bother you again, but I think there are a couple of things I would like you to know, regardless of how insignificant they may be.
(...)
I must admit I was somewhat hurt by your saying that one way or another - even if inadvertently - I had to be a spy. More accurately, I was not really hurt by your saying that since I can well understand your doubts, but by the process of thinking that had presumably led you to such a conclusion. As you will probably admit, had I never sent you my asylum statement, you would have written the endorsement of my application that I had asked you for with no hesitation. In a way then, your suspicions about the possibility of my being a spy were aroused by my trying to be as honest with you as possible.
(...)
Clearly, there are now two possibilities: either you think that I am a "full-bloodied" spy, acting with absolute premeditation, or that I inadvertently passed on information to my interrogators in the course of my prolonged encounters with them. If you believe the former, there is nothing I can say or do that would convince you otherwise. If, however, you tend to think that the latter is the case, then it seems to me that you underestimate the extreme polarization of political views that has occurred in Poland. "Inadvertent spying" is practically impossible in a country where any "sitting on the fence" is morally far more reprehensible than proclaiming one's total adherence to either the pro or the anti-government forces.. The determination of people on both sides of the barricade is carried to such extremes that it is quite possible to stare at the faces of your interrogators for years without actually divulging any significant information whatsoever.
(...)
I hope you will treat this letter as a friendly gesture. Most of what I said above has no longer any immediate importance. Whatever your feelings about me may be, I do hope you will remember me as someone you met in Poland at a very interesting time.

Woodward never responded, but that was to be expected.

On October the 8th 1984 political asylum was granted by the Department of State - Lucy, Jakub, and I were on our way to become Americans, although that process took another 6 years. During that time we were using strange, government issued documents which looked like passports, except they were white, and on the front cover they had an inscription saying "This is not a US passport". They were in effect travel documents which allowed us to leave the country and then come back without the usual visa hassle. In one of the pages there was a box titled "Nationality" and it said "Stateless". It was a strange feeling to have a would-be passport which proclaimed that you belonged to no country in the world.

By the time we became US citizens, Poland regained full independence and started a long process of recovery, but for us it was already too late. We established various contacts, both professional and personal, gained new friends, had another child, our daughter Karolina, and - generally speaking - made America our new home.

Neither Polish nor American authorities ever contacted me in the US after I got my asylum. And, sadly, I was never again hooked up to a lie detector. There was one brief contact between me and an FBI agent. Apparently all newly minted asylees have to have an interview with a representative of federal authorities. In my case a special agent, who happened to be a young and very polite woman, showed up at our apartment and spent half an hour asking me pointless questions to which the Bureau had proper answers anyway. Ever since then I was left alone.

As for Ziggy, for the first two years after my emigration he seemed to be under the impression that whatever was happening to me in America was in some way a clever ploy and that at any time I will show up back in Poland, ready to divulge all kinds of important information. Every now and then he called by parents, introduced himself as a "colleague from work", and asked whether there was any news about the date of my coming back. By that time my father knew exactly who he was, but played this game for as long as it was possible. But one day Ziggy called once more and asked the same question again. This time my dad answered: "Listen, I know who you are, I know you are not my son's colleague, and you know he is never coming back. So get lost". Ziggy never called again.

A few months after the asylum decision I attended a seminar taught by a well-known female professor who specialized in the subject of feminism. For reasons unknown, in one of these sessions I entered into a discussion with her (maybe even an argument) about the notion of freedom. The professor expressed the view that the freedoms Americans were supposed to enjoy were largely illusory and heavily dependent on social status, gender, and wealth. She was certainly right to some extent, but I - a fresh escapee from the communist world - couldn't quite acquiesce. I believed then, as I believe now, that the difference between western socialism and Soviet socialism is more or less the same as the difference between a chair and an electric chair. The same goes for the concept of freedom.

A journalist talks to Polish prime minister.

"The latest public opinion polls suggest that the majority of Poles are happy with their lives and their current situation"

"So what's the problem?"

"These Poles live in the United States"

Postcard no. 25 - Postscript

It has been 40 years since I left my country and became an emigre. In those years there have been enormous changes on both sides of the Atlantic. In 2014 Lucy and I traveled with our London friends, Sue and Louis, back to Poland, this time to its eastern part, and ended up in the city of Gdańsk where just a few days earlier president Barack Obama congratulated the Polish people on the 25th anniversary of regaining full independence. For the Poles it was an amazing quarter of a century during which they successfully transitioned to a democratic society, largely integrated with Western Europe.

I never expected this to happen in my lifetime, and I was certainly not alone. But it did happen, and watching Poland from afar, succeeding in various respects and shedding the 4-decade baggage of totalitarian rule has been very exciting. Usually there are all sorts of questions asked of people who decided to emigrate, but whose countries then suddenly changed in such a way that emigration seemed unnecessary. One of these questions is invariably this: "Would you considering going back?". I wouldn't, but I am sure very many other emigres might have different opinions or might be hesitant about what to do.

Another question often asked is about loyalties and patriotism. I have never been a patriot in the traditional sense of the term and I try to stay away from "show off" patriotic spectacles which usually are just a step away from nationalism. So, no nostalgic imagery of weeping willows along the banks of the Vistula River for me. Today I view Poland very much like Chicago Bears fans view the players of their team - they root for them, and they want them to succeed, whatever the odds, but they obviously don't want to be a part of their game.

As I was flying out of the Warsaw airport in 1983, it was with a conviction that this was a "forever" move, and that there was no going back. I stayed true to that conviction, for example by keeping away from participating in any way in Polish elections, both before the fall of communism or after, even though I had the right do so. My feeling has always been that when someone decides to become a citizen of a new country, he or she should relinquish any right to have a voice in the political future of the old one.

When I talk to other emigres, both in the US and elsewhere, some of them say that somehow their lives under totalitarianism amounted to just wasted time. I do not share this opinion. It is true that every now and then the insanity and hardship of daily existence was overwhelming and depressing. But without all these experiences, without some incredible friends and memories associated with them, we would have all been dramatically different people.

In recent years America went through some turbulent and potentially dangerous events which to some extent threatened the democratic roots of the nation more than previous dramatic upheavals, such as the civil war, two world wars or the attacks of 9/11. I have been at times both astonished and disappointed to see how Americans take what they have for granted and how they never even consider the possibility of losing their freedoms. This is a grave and precarious mistake. There are countries that relatively recently lost their democratic systems of government, e.g. Venezuela, Brazil, and Hungary. In fact, Poland was on the verge of sharing the same fate, because of the election of populist, nationalistic government which ruled for 8 years. Thankfully, these people were removed from power in 2013, mostly by young and female voters. Nothing is guaranteed for life unless you are ready to stand up for it, and it is great that the Polish electorate awoke from its political slumber just in time. And with that I end my secular pontification.

Looking today at some of the archival footage from PRL, its

comic aspects are obvious, because East European communism was to a large extent a farce of amazing proportions. And yet it was our lives, and at times all of this stuff was deadly serious. The people who took power in Poland at the end of the war, and who took orders from Moscow, destroyed the lives of millions of people and kept the country in the state of horrible stagnation for over 40 years. Eventually, however, they failed miserably, and today's Poland is a great testimony to that failure.

Another testimony to that failure is Ziggy. If he is still among the living, he must be well into his 80s, and I am sure he no longer chases potential British spies. Unfortunately, thousands of people like him served the communist security apparatus and enforced the will of the rulers. They usually worked diligently until the very end, and then thought that somehow they would continue as before in the new Poland which they worked against. It didn't happen that way, and it shouldn't have.

I owe a debt of gratitude to countless family members and friends in Europe and America who were and are participants, often unwitting ones, in my journey. Today I sometimes wonder about how it was at all possible for a kid from Zduny in People's Republic of Poland to end up in American suburbia. And how come I now live relatively comfortably in the state of Indiana, with my spouse of 700 hundred years and two dogs. And how it happened that I have two great, grown-up children, born on opposite sides of the Atlantic. What can possibly explain this trajectory? The problem is that I really don't know.

Milton Keynes UK
Ingram Content Group UK Ltd.
UKHW050757020124
435290UK00010B/102

9 781088 180495